Praise for *Artful*

Jackie Kay's Book of the Year for 2013,
*The Guardian* (London)

"These brief, acrobatic lectures . . . perform spectacular feats of
criticism. Each is as playful as it is powerful, as buoyant as it is
brilliant."                                               —*NPR Books*

"A wordsmith to the very smithy of her soul, [Smith] is at once
deeply playful and deeply serious. And her new book, in which she
tugs at God's sleeve, ruminates on clowns, shoplifts used books,
dabbles in Greek, and palavers with the dead, is a stunner."
                                    —*The New York Times Book Review*

"Ms. Smith has an agile and mischievous mind. I will keep this
book on my shelves forever. . . . It's a book with unusual nooks and
crannies, a book that pulses with minor-chord heartache. . . .
What matters in both life and literature, this book suggests, is to
keep trying to connect." —Dwight Garner, *The New York Times*

"What a treat . . . *Artful* is a love story full of everything—mind
and body, past, present, and future. The last lines of this wonderful book are spoken by the narrator: '(Who did I think I was talking to? You.)' Thank you, Ali Smith, from all of us."
                                            —*San Francisco Chronicle*

"Smith dealt before with grief in relation to the passing of time in
her 2001 novel, *Hotel World*. The clever structure on show in *Artful* allows her to expand on this theme and enables the reader to
delve back in at random and be entranced all over again."
                                            —*Minneapolis Star Tribune*

"A moving dialogue between people and genres . . . *Artful* is a
charming balancing act."                       —*Financial Times*

"One of the marvelous things about this book is its reconciliation
of the serious—both in the form of this crumbling, smelly guest

and in its ardent advocacy of art—and light. Smith, whose love of words and skill at wordplay has already been made apparent in her stories and novels, performs dodge after dodge after dodge. . . . What Smith has done with *Artful* is to invent a new form apart from form, to build a kind of Frankenstein's monster inside the act of art."                     —*Los Angeles Review of Books*

"*Artful* is full of crossings and parallels. It is thought in 3-D. It is artful, which the book itself observes is the name given to the Oliver Twist character of the Dodger: the one who animates the story, who brings life to it."                     —*St. Louis Post-Dispatch*

"Contemplative, electrifying, and transformative . . . Through riveting reflections on the limitations and the limitlessness of stories, Smith considers four aspects of the endeavor of creation: on 'time,' 'form,' 'edge,' and 'offer and reflection.' The results are redemptive for everyone, testifying with singular clarity and wit to the immutable necessity for art."
                    —*Publishers Weekly* (starred review)

"[An] extraordinary journey . . . Smith's storytelling facility and critical eye are evident in the fact that this ongoing conversation about time, memory, loss, longing, love, art and nature stirs the mind and heart all the more because it takes place between the imagination and reality. A soulful intellectual inquiry and reflection on life and art, artfully done."                     —*Kirkus Reviews*

"Smith daringly splits herself into two captivating voices. . . . This scintillating conversation showcases Smith's own gifts as a creative writer. But it also reminds readers of how great literature—of Shakespeare, Lawrence, Hopkins, Ovid, Plath, Rilke, and Flaubert—requires them to reorient their line of vision. Nothing—Smith shows her reader—forces such reorientation more than violating conventional boundaries, often in dangerous ways. These most unlecture-like of lectures deliver the thrill of perilous border crossings."                     —*Booklist*

PENGUIN BOOKS

# ARTFUL

Ali Smith is the author of nine works of fiction, including the novel *Hotel World*, which won the Encore Award and the Scottish Arts Council Book of the Year Award, and *The Accidental*, which won the Whitbread Award and was shortlisted for the Man Booker Prize and the Orange Broadband Prize for Fiction. Her story collections include *Free Love* and *The Whole Story and Other Stories*. Her most recent novel, *There But For The*, was named one of *The Guardian*'s Best Books of 2011 and NPR's Five 2011 books That Stay with You. Born in Inverness, Scotland, Smith now lives in Cambridge, United Kingdom.

# Artful

# Ali
# Smith

PENGUIN BOOKS

PENGUIN BOOKS
Published by the Penguin Group
Penguin Group (USA) LLC
375 Hudson Street
New York, New York 10014

USA | Canada | UK | Ireland | Australia
New Zealand | India | South Africa | China
penguin.com
A Penguin Random House Company

First published in Great Britain by Hamish Hamilton,
an imprint of Penguin Books Ltd., 2012
First published in the United States of America by The Penguin Press,
a member of Penguin Group (USA) Inc., 2013
Published in Penguin Books 2014

THE LIBRARY OF CONGRESS HAS CATALOGED THE HARDCOVER EDITION AS FOLLOWS:
Smith, Ali.
Artful / Ali Smith.
pages    cm
Originally presented as four lectures for the Weidenfeld
Visiting Professorship in European comparative literature at
St Anne's College, Oxford, in January and February 2012.
Includes bibliographical references.
ISBN 978-1-59420-486-9 (hc.)
ISBN 978-0-14-312449-8 (pbk.)
1. Literature—History and criticism—Theory, etc.   2. Comparative
literature.   3. Authorship.   I. Title.
PN441.S585       2013
809—dc23

Printed in the United States of America
5   7   9   10   8   6   4

*Designed by Marysarah Quinn*

This book began life as four lectures given for the Weidenfeld Visiting Professorship in European Comparative Literature at St. Anne's College, Oxford, in January and February 2012. The lectures are published here pretty much as they were delivered.

I owe a great debt of thanks to everyone at St. Anne's for making this book happen at all, and for looking after me there with such care, cleverness, and grace. Huge thanks for their kindness to Tim Gardam, Sally Shuttleworth, Matthew Reynolds, and Lord Weidenfeld.

Don't try to hold on to the wave
That's breaking against your foot: so long as
You stand in the stream fresh waves
Will always keep breaking against it.

BERTOLT BRECHT

translated by Gerhard Nellhaus

# Contents

On time | *1*

On form | *49*

On edge | *97*

On offer and on reflection | *153*

Some sources | *223*

# Artful

# On time

'The wind doth blow today, my love,
　　And a few small drops of rain;
　　I never had but one true-love,
　　　In cold grave she was lain.
'I'll do as much for my true-love
　　As any young man may;
　I'll sit and mourn all at her grave
　　For a twelvemonth and a day.'

The twelvemonth and a day being up, I was still at a
loss. If anything I was more at a loss.

So I went and stood in our study and looked at your
desk, where the unfinished stuff, what you'd been working on last, was still neatly piled. I looked at your books,
I took one of your books off a shelf at random—*my* study,
*my* desk, *my* books, now.

The book I took down today happened actually to
have been one of mine originally. It was a Dickens novel,

Oliver Twist, the old Penguin edition I'd had at university, with a spine whose orange had almost completely faded and a jolly engraving of drunks and children in a pub on the cover, which was beginning to peel away from the spine. It would probably stand one more read. I'd not read Oliver Twist since, oh god, when? way before we even first knew each other, I'd had to, for university, so that made it thirty years.

That gave me a shake. A twelvemonth and a day can arguably be called short, but thirty years? How could thirty years be the blink-of-the-eye it felt? It was the difference between black and white footage of the Second World War and David Bowie on Top of the Pops singing Life on Mars; it was the size of a grown woman with four children, one of them nearly old enough, if the woman started very early, to be doing A-levels. They definitely weren't called A-levels any more.

Maybe I might try to read Oliver Twist, the whole thing, from start to finish. I hadn't read anything, I hadn't been able to, for well over a twelvemonth and a day. I opened the book at chapter 1, page 45, which *Treats of the Place where Oliver Twist was Born, and of the Circumstances attending his Birth* (that's quite a lot of pages before he was even born, forty-four. But I didn't really want to read someone's introduction, my introduction days were over thank god; there are some good things about getting a bit older), and I sat down in the armchair by the window.

There was a draft by this window. There'd always been a draft by this window because one year when we painted it then left it a little open to dry we couldn't get it to close completely again without cracking the paint, and you never wanted to crack it because you'd painted it so carefully, so we never did. I knew that if I sat there for any length of time I'd end up with a really sore neck and shoulder even though right now it was summer. Summer: a couple of times in the twelvemonth and a day I'd wondered if the seasons would ever be new again, brand-new time, rather than just seem to be following each other nose to tail like paint-peeling wooden horses on an old carousel.

I looked across the room to the other window, where I'd always thought it would be better to have that chair anyway. The light would be better there and it also happened to be closer to the desk, which meant I'd be able to angle the anglepoise and carry on reading when it got dark.

But it was your chair, this chair, even though we'd

bought it on my credit card (and it still wasn't paid off; how unfair that a chair we saw online and bought on a credit card and had delivered in a van would, could, did, last longer than us). And we'd had the argument about moving it several times and you'd always won that argument.

I think it was the thought of the extra day past the twelvemonth, a single new day on top of the heap of gone days, gone months. I dropped the book onto the seat of the chair and I started dragging the chair across the room.

It was heavy, much heavier than it looked, so I stopped halfway and stood behind it and pushed. Partly the pushing was difficult too because one of the rugs caught under it and got dragged across the room and I had the feeling I was maybe scuffing the floorboards quite badly with one of its legs, yes I was, look, I could see a gouge appearing beneath me as I pushed. But it was my floor, I could do what I liked to it, so I kept pushing even though the rug was still rucked up under it and all the other rugs in the room had messed up too.

I got my breath back and I picked up that book again, mine, not yours, and sat down in the chair in its new place; it opened at a picture of a boy down on the ground and another standing as if he's just punched him, a woman at the open door aghast, another holding the small boy back from punching again. The words underneath said *Oliver plucks up a Spirit*. Yes, the light was much better here. The rugs, all skewy now, looked like creatures, a mess of dogs asleep in random places on the floor. I quite liked that. I liked the thought that the room was full of new and unexpected sleeping dogs.

Among other public buildings in a certain town which for many reasons it will be prudent to refrain from mentioning, and to which I will assign no fictitious name, it boasts of one which is common to most towns, great or small, to wit, a workhouse; and in this workhouse was born, on a day and date which I need not take upon myself to repeat, inasmuch as it can be of no possible consequence to the reader, in this stage of the business at all events, the item of mortality whose name is prefixed to the head of this chapter. For a long time after he was ushered into this world of sorrow and trouble, by the parish surgeon, it remained a matter of considerable doubt whether the child would survive to bear any name at all; in which case it is somewhat more than probable that these memoirs would never have appeared, or, if they had, being comprised within a couple of pages, that they would have possessed the inestimable merit of being the most concise and faithful specimen of biography extant in the literature of any age or country.

First: why wouldn't Dickens name the town this was happening in? Then: the word workhouse reminded me of my father telling me once that at one point his mother (my grandmother) worked in a workhouse laundry. That's how close this anywhere of a place was to me now all those years in the future. Then: how can a birthday mean nothing? Then: a reminder that time will tell. Then this phrase: item of mortality: three words that mean a baby, a person; more—the item of mortality could mean the whole book, like I was somehow holding an item of mortality in my hands. Then: this world of sorrow. When I read those words I felt again the weight of my own sorrow, the world I carried on my own back; and at exactly the same time the fact that someone somewhere sometime else had thought of the world as a world of sorrow too made the weight on my own back feel a bit better.

Was that a knocking? someone at the front door? No, whatever it was, it stopped. It was probably next door: they'd probably heard me moving the chair and decided to do some rivalrous moving-things-about.

I went back to the book. A matter of considerable doubt whether the child would survive to bear any name at all: this was interesting. Was being named a proof of survival? Without a name would something live less long? for instance, be doomed to being only a couple of pages long? And was naming to do with survival, and were both naming and survival also somehow both to do with time?

There, I thought. I'm okay. I've moved a really heavy chair. I've changed things. And I've read sixteen lines in a novel and I've thought several things about them and none of this with you, or to do with you; I even read the phrase 'item of mortality' and thought of something other than you. Time heals all wounds. Or, as you used to say, time achilles-heels all wounds. Then you would tell the story of Achilles's mother dipping him in the protective river, holding him by the heel between her finger and thumb; that's why the heel got missed out, didn't get protected. Which, you said, when it came to story, was what suspense meant. And from then on all time's arrows pointed at that unprotected heel.

Except, I don't always have to be thinking about what you used to say. In fact I just managed a whole ten minutes there without thinking of you once, I thought, then I turned back to the book. Then I looked up over the top of the open book because it sounded like someone was coming up the stairs.

Someone was. It was you.

You were standing in the doorway. You coughed. The cough was you in a way that couldn't not be you.

You were covered in dust and what looked like bits of rubble. Your clothes were smudged, matted, torn. You were wearing that black waistcoat with the white stitching that went out of fashion in 1995, the one we gave to Oxfam. Your skin was smudged. Your hair was streaked with dust and grit. You looked bruised. You shook yourself slightly there on the landing and little bits of grit and rubble fell off you, I watched some of it fall down the stairs behind you.

I'm late, you said.

You're—, I said.

Late, you said again and brushed at your arms and shoulders. I'm later than—. I'm later than—. Than—.

You're later than a rabbit in Alice, I said because that's what you'd always said when you were late.

Than a what, in what? you said.

A rabbit, I said. In Alice.

What's that, again? you said.

You put your hand to your head as if to find your glasses but there were no glasses there.

From Alice in Wonderland, I said. The White Rabbit. It carries a pocket watch. Remember? It's always checking the time.

What time is it, again? you said.

I got my phone out of my pocket.

Quarter to eight, I said.

Then I realized I'd misheard you and what you'd actually said was: *what is it, again, time?*

It was you except for at the eyes. Where they'd been, a blue like no one else's, there were now black spaces. It looked like your whole eyes had become pupil. You stepped into the room like you were blind. Leaving a trail of rubbly stuff very like what I'd had in my hand when we all stood round and I threw the urnful of you up and down the old Roman road in the wood on the path that's lined with the beech trees, you went through and stood in front of your own old desk, all the papers piled on it pretty much the way you left them.

Then you groaned, stepped back and went through to the front room, left the doors all open behind you. You sat down in front of the off television.

You came back from the dead to watch tv? I said.

You didn't say anything. I switched it on. You sat slumped in front of the looped footage on BBC 24 of a few young people in hoods loping about in a hunched way in front of a Debenhams. The announcers talked about riots and people phoned in sounding outraged over footage which repeated itself, then repeated itself again. Then I noticed that the phone-in people's voices were also on repeat.

I sat with you, watching you watch it for half an hour. Then I thought maybe I should offer you a cup of tea. But wasn't there some folklore rule about not giving the dead food, or not accepting food from them? Well, but this was you. And also, obviously, it wasn't you; this was my imagination. I could offer a figment of my imagination tea if I wanted.

I went through to the kitchen and made one—milk, one sugar—in the mug you'd liked best. I brought it through and handed it to you. I went over to the tv to find the remote and when I looked round you had upended the mug and were pouring the hot tea out onto the floor. Then you put the empty mug in your pocket.

There was a report on about the 1991 Gulf War, about the epidemic of cancer in children all across Iraq which was still happening today, twenty years later, because the US military had used missiles and bullets coated in depleted uranium, sending a dust through the country which *will still be radioactive*, the voice-over was saying, *four thousand five hundred million years from now*. It was the kind of thing you'd have been incensed about, you'd have been jumping up and down in your chair about.

Now I know for sure you're not real, I said.

You turned your black eyes on me.

What is it, again, real? you said.

I switched the tv off.

Okay, I said. As long as I've got you here, we're going to use and appreciate this present moment. Because I wish, and I've wished a thousand times since you went, that we'd known it was the present, and that we were living in it.

You reached over and picked up the pencil sharpener from off the table at the side of the sofa.

So, there are two things I've wanted to tell you, I said.

You turned the sharpener over in your hand then dropped it into the pocket of your waistcoat. I heard it clink in there against the mug.

Well, a lot more than two, but these are the two that

I've wanted most to tell you, I said. Actually, the first is something I wanted to show you.

I went through to the study, to the bookshelf, to the J's, reached up and got down Volume 1 of your old 1909 copy of Henry James's The Golden Bowl. Back in the spring when I'd decided I'd try to read again I'd chosen this book, partly because you loved it. You particularly loved this copy, which you'd found in a charity shop and bought both volumes of for £4.00. I'd sat in the garden with it in my first spring for a quarter of a century without you and I'd tried to read it. But reading was one of the things I couldn't do. On the day I'd decided was going to be the last day of me trying, I'd opened it at random and had remembered this: you rushing out of the garden and into the kitchen a couple of summers ago with the book open going, look! look at this! it's probably a hundred years old, a hundred-year-old greenfly, it could literally be a hundred years since anyone's opened this, look at its wings! you can actually see the veins, you can actually still see the green of it, think, a hundred years ago this greenfly could've been visiting hundred-year-ago roses, what about that, isn't it a total beauty?

Page 338, I said now.

I opened it, carried it across and put it on your knee.

I pointed to the word *from*, quite high up on the page, round which the greenfly, wings splayed, still very lightly green after all the years, was.

See? I said.

You held the book, looked at it, looked at me, bewildered.

Anyway, I said, taking the book back and shutting it and putting it on the arm of the chair, the second of the two things I've most wanted to tell you.

What's two, again? you said.

I pulled my jumper up and showed you, over my left hip, my tattoo.

This is the story of my tattoo. When we are first lovers, I tell you I want to get a tattoo. You tell me you hate tattoos, you think they're cheap and that you don't want me to have one. You say you think their historical precedent, after a century like the twentieth, means tattoos are now forever an indelible sign of a kind of brutality, and you ask me do I know what indelible means and how difficult they are to remove. I tell you I'm going to get one whether you like it or not, and that I want a tattoo of William Blake's tiger on my shoulder and you say, what, the whole poem? you'll have to make sure the tattooist knows to spell it with a y. I say no, not the poem, I want the picture he did of the tiger he wrote the poem about. You laugh out loud and tell me what Angela Carter said about that 'fubsy beast'; she thought he looked more like a pajama case than a tiger. I go away and look up the word fubsy. I've never heard it before.

The next night I tell you I've decided that I'll only have a tattoo done if you choose what it's going to be.

Right, you say, I know exactly what.

You go to your bookshelves (this is before we're living together, before we do the most faithful act of all, mix our separate books into one library) and you take down a slim volume of Jane Austen, open it and flick through it till you find what you're looking for.

From there, you say, to there.

I didn't know there was earlier Jane Austen than Pride and Prejudice and Sense and Sensibility. This is from something I've never heard of called Jack & Alice. I read it:

The perfect form, the beautifull face, & elegant manners of Lucy so won on the affections of Alice that when they parted, which was not till after Supper, she assured her that except her Father, Brother, Uncles, Aunts, Cousins & other relations, Lady Williams,

Charles Adams & a few dozen more of particular freinds, she loved her better than almost any other person in the world.

Okay, which bit do you want? I say.

All of it, you say, from *The* to *world*, and I'll expect your tattooist to spell beautiful like Austen does, with two l's, and friend like the young Austen did, with its i and its e the other way round, f r e i n and d. Or you'll need to get yourself a new skin because nothing less will do for me if you're so determined to have a tattoo. Okay?

All of it? I say.

Lucky for you the ands are ampersands, you say.

You are calling my bluff, of course. I call yours back. I take that book to the tattoo parlor down Mill Road and I come home, after several sessions, with exactly this tattoo. I choose to have it done in deep blue, the color of your eyes. It costs me a fortune. It hurts like irony.

I see you again only when it's finished and my skin's settled down.

You're unreal, you say when you see it. You're the real unreal thing all right.

Less than a month after this we move in together and mix our books up.

Now I stood in front of the phantom you with my shirt pulled up so you with your deep black eyes were level with my hip bone.

Since you went, I say, I've almost slept with just one other person. I don't know why I did, I was lonely, I suppose, and I was going a bit mad. Anyway, this person, she opened my shirt, you know, we were about to, and she looked at my tattoo and she said: did you know they've spelt the word beautiful wrong on your tattoo. And she didn't even bother to read down as far as the word freind, to comment on that. So I buttoned up my shirt again and I made up an excuse and I left.

You looked at my hip bone then you looked up at me and for the first time since you'd come back I thought I saw something like recognition cross your face.

*That's* what two is again, you said.

\*

The twelvemonth and a day being up,
The dead began to speak:
'Oh who sits weeping on my grave,
And will not let me sleep?'
"Tis I, my love, sits on your grave,
And will not let you sleep;

For I crave one kiss of your clay-cold lips,
And that is all I seek.'

## 1: You Must Remember This : why we have time and why time has us

What's the quickest short story in the world? Once upon a time gentlemen please. What would a place without time be like? Maybe a bit like George Mackay Brown describes Tir-Nan-Og, the land of eternal youth 'far in the west,' where

> there was no sickness or withering or suffering or death. Always the fields were heavy and gold with harvest, always the orchards were laden with apples; all the stones were precious. No storms beat about the ships and the doors of the people. The people of *Tir-Nan-Og* were themselves young and beautiful for ever, with no ashes in the beard or in the long lissom golden hair of a girl.

It'd never work. It'd be like being dead and not knowing it. We'd pick up one stone after another and they'd all be

the boring precious same. We'd have to invent leafless-
ness, imagine harvest failure. Then we'd invent time.
And as soon as we did, everything would become meaningful and the first gray hairs would appear and until
they did we'd probably feign death just so we could tell
stories about it.

Walter Benjamin says that's where the storyteller's
authority comes from, death. Joseph Conrad, in his 1917
novel, The Shadow-Line, sees a lack of time as a state of
absolute childishness, where only 'the very young have,
properly speaking, no moments.' Time means. Time will
tell. It's consequence, suspense, morality, mortality. Box-
ers fight in bouts between bells ringing time. Prisoners
do time. Time's just 'one damn thing after another,' Margaret Atwood says. That sounds like conventional narrative plot. And at the end of our allotted time, we'll end
up in one of those, a conventional plot I mean, unless
we stipulate otherwise in our wills. From one will to another, to Shakespeare, and his thoughts on Devouring
Time, Time's pencil, Time's fell and injurious hand,
Time's scythe, Time's fickle glass: 'Ruin hath taught me
thus to ruminate / That Time will come and take my love
away.' The first line, in its conscious rhetoric and with its
internal rhyme, its alliterating, its assonance, its thus-

ing, is literally undone by the next line, the thud of mono-syllable after monosyllable eight times before the word away. Time will undo us. Sometimes we don't want it to, sometimes we do. 'O time, thou must untangle this, not I. It is too hard a knot for me t'untie,' Viola says, trans-formed into her own dead brother in Twelfth Night, be-fore the whirligig of time brings in his revenges and the plot, having thickened, finally thins.

Is it time that translates our lives into sequence, into meaning? Does sequence mean that things mean? Se-quence will always be most of the word consequence. José Saramago in his memoir, Small Memories (translated by Margaret Jull Costa), recalls being ten years old when his grandmother died; he specifically remembers this time of his child self's coming to consciousness by a linkage of clocks and death:

My mother turned up one morning at the school in Lago do Leão to bring the unfortunate news. She had come to fetch me, perhaps following some social con-vention of which I knew nothing, but which, appar-ently, on the death of a grandparent, required the grandchildren to be brought home at once. I remem-ber glancing up at the clock on the wall in the en-

trance hall above the door, and thinking, like someone
making a conscious effort to collect information that
might prove useful to him in future, that I should
make a note of the time. I seem to recall that it was a
few minutes past ten.

A few minutes past ten years old, Saramago is writing
this in his eighties. 'Make use of a short daylight,' Katherine Mansfield says in a letter well before she's ill, before
she's had any real inkling that she might not last past
the middle of her thirties. 'Disegnia antonio disegnia
antonio / disegnia e non perdere tempo': draw antonio
draw antonio / draw and don't waste time—Michelangelo
wrote these words to his boy apprentice on some studies
of the Virgin and Child (except what he really wrote, because he wrote it so fast, was 'disegnia e no prder tepo' or
draw and dnt wast tim). It's one of the most repeated
themes in Michelangelo's poetry (translated here by
Christopher Ryan) that no matter the art, no matter the
love, no matter the money, 'whoever is born arrives at
death through time's swift passage; and the sun leaves
nothing alive . . . our ancient lineages are as shadows to
the sun . . . Once our eyes were fully formed, shining in

both sockets; now these are empty, horrible and black: such is the work of time.'

Michelangelo lived to be nearly three times as old as Mansfield, who shared his knowledge, like Damien Hirst does, like all artists do, that regardless of how precious the stones stuck all over it are, it's a skull—and regardless of whether it's the 1520s in the sun in Florence or the first decade of the twenty-first century in an aesthetically reproduced Scandinavian sunrise in a London art gallery, you must remember this, as time goes by, the fundamental things apply.

## 2: I'm in Pieces, Bits and Pieces : the fragmentation imagination (could call it the imfragmentation? the imfragination??? NB)

'But it is only in ashes that a story endures, / Nothing persists except extinguished things,' Montale says (or Edwin Morgan does, translating Montale). The earliest story we have, The Epic of Gilgamesh—and we only actually have pieces of it, we're still finding and rearranging the pieces, written on ancient baked tablets, of this proof, this broken indication of the countless literatures of the past lost to us—is about what happens when a man's friend goes into the House of Dust, 'the house which none who enters ever leaves.'

Enkidu, Gilgamesh's friend, grows ill and dies. 'How can I keep silent? How can I stay quiet? / My friend, whom I loved, has turned to clay.' Gilgamesh mourns him, in one of the most beautiful poetic elegies that yet exist, then immediately goes on a journey to find eternal life so the same thing won't happen to him. When he fails to snare the source of living forever he returns home to the city of which he's king and builds a statue instead to commemorate his dead friend. He accepts his own mortality. He puts aside his tyrannous ways; reforms his morality. He remakes his friend, in clay.

'Decay is the beginning of all birth,' as Paracelsus has it, 'the midwife of very great things.' This is Czesław Miłosz on decay, from his poem called No More (translated by Anthony Miłosz):

if I could find for their miserable bones
In a graveyard whose gates are licked by greasy water
A word more enduring than their last-used comb
That in the rot under tombstones, alone, awaits the light,

Then I wouldn't doubt. Out of reluctant matter
What can be gathered? Nothing, beauty at best.
And so, cherry blossoms must suffice for us
And chrysanthemums and the full moon.

Miłosz conjures not just the real mutable things which will have to 'suffice for us,' and not just the poet's act of finding the images for these things, but the poet's vital quest for a word that will 'last,' an art which will last longer than the things we quotidianly use in our lives without thinking for a minute they'll survive us, or that they might be all that survives of us—the word which won't just record our brevity, but will stand as a paradox, beyond transience, for our essential transience.

A late poem by Edwin Morgan, The Sandal, does the same thing but this time *for* a poet, and almost as a revelation that art itself is a broken thing if it's anything, and that the act of remaking, or imagining, or imaginative involvement, is what makes the difference:

What is this picture but a fragment?
Is it linen—papyrus—who can say?
All those stains and fents and stretched bits, but

she was a character, even a beauty, you can see that

from the set of her head and the rakish snood

her tight black curls are fighting to escape from.

She is wearing a very very pale violet tunic

which is partly transparent, partly translucent,

partly not there. It has slipped off one shoulder

but the shoulder is gone. The other arm has faded

to a scarcely perceptible gesture. One sandal

gleams. All the rest is conjecture.

Her name is a letter or two: Sa, Saf—

O she is all fragments. There she is though!

As Matthew Reynolds says in The Poetry of Translation, about Sappho and the fragments that are all we have of her love poetry, 'the longing represented in the fragments was doubled by a longing felt by readers for the fragments themselves to be made whole.' It's the act of making it up, from the combination of what we've got and what we haven't, that makes the human, makes the art, makes this transformation possible, like it's the eye engaged in the creative act, in union with a kind of <u>not</u> seeing, in Rilke's poem Archaic Torso of Apollo (translated here by Stephen Mitchell):

We cannot know his legendary head
with eyes like ripening fruit. And yet his torso
is still suffused with brilliance from inside,
like a lamp, in which his gaze, now turned to low,

gleams in all its power. Otherwise
the curved breast could not dazzle you so, nor could
a smile run through the placid hips and thighs
to that dark center where procreation flared.

Otherwise this stone would seem defaced
beneath the translucent cascade of the shoulders
and would not glisten like a wild beast's fur:

would not, from all the borders of itself,
burst like a star: for here there is no place
that does not see you. You must change your life.

The first thing the imagining eye does is supply what's not there, giving the statue not just a head but a legendary one; its missing eyes are both seen ('like ripening fruit') and at the same time never seeable ('we cannot know'). It's the fact that Apollo <u>does not have</u> 'his legendary head' that gives the torso, all there is left, the explicit, newly muted 'gaze,' that gives the smile to the hips and thighs, that heals the defacement. In its own literal face-off, in a magical shifting of the position of observer and observed, it means that the 'you' of the poem becomes not just the seen thing instead of the art, but something seen so utterly, so wholly, that 'there is no place that does not see you.' It's this being seen (met in the act of looking)—the exchange that happens when art and human meet—that results in the pure urgency for transformation: 'you must change your life.'

Which is all very well if your missing head's a god-head. Wisława Szymborska's observer in her poem Greek Statue (translated by Clare Cavanagh and Stanisław Barańczak) is much more sanguine. The dismembered statue, the speaker says, with all the bits, the arms, legs, genitals, head, knocked off it by time, is bloody lucky, never having been alive in the first place: 'When someone living dies that way / blood flows at every blow.' To Szymborska though, still, the remains act as a revelation of 'all the grace and gravity / of what was lost.'

Time's an old song. (Three wheels on my wagon / and I'm still rolling along / The Cherokees / are chasing me / arrows fly / right on by / but I'm singing a happy song . . . Then: Two wheels on my wagon / But I'm still rolling along . . . Then: One wheel on my wagon . . . Then: No wheels on my wagon . . .) All songs involve time, because music depends on time. Time's a song against the clock, sometimes a happy one, sometimes not, like The Unquiet Grave, a Child Ballad from the early fifteenth century where a lover mourns on the grave of a lost love 'for a twelvemonth and a day' only to be told by the ghost to go away, stop bothering the dead, get a life before it's too late. 'You crave one kiss of my clay-cold lips; / But my breath smells earthy strong; / If you have one kiss of my clay-cold lips, / Your time will not be long.'


## 3: If They Asked Me, I Could Write a Book

'In a novel there is always a clock,' as EM Forster says in Aspects of the Novel. Forster called time (and narrative's interwoven union with it) the 'interminable tapeworm.' He thought the novelist ought to—had to—grasp the 'thread' of it: thread is a great word here, calling to mind yet more worms, *and* the three fates with their scissors ready to cut us off at the end of our stamina when the life story's all sewn up. Nowadays thread has an altogether new virtual meaning, has become a column of recorded information that has the appearance of instantaneity and is probably really out of date. And when I think of Forster's tapeworm I can't help thinking of the Nicola Barker short story Symbiosis: Class Cestoda, where a girl takes her boyfriend, Sean, out to a restaurant to tell him she's fallen in love with her own tapeworm and is leaving him and settling down with the worm instead.

The difference between the short story form and the novel form is to do, not with length, but with time. The short story will always be about brevity, 'The shortness of life! The shortness of life!' (as one of Mansfield's characters in her story At the Bay can't help but exclaim). Because of this, the short story can do anything it likes with notions of time; it moves and works spatially regardless of whether it adheres to chronology or conventional plot. It is an elastic form; it can be as imagistic and achronological as it likes and it will still hold its form. In this it emphasizes the momentousness of the moment. At the same time it deals in, and doesn't compromise on, the purely momentary nature of everything, both timeless *and* transient.

The story can be partial, can be a piece of something

and still hold its own, still be whole. The novel, on the other hand, is bound to and helplessly interested in society and social hierarchy, in social worlds; and society is always attached to, in debt to, made by and revealed by the trappings of its time. And the novel is bound to be linear, even if it's a rearranged BS Johnson work—even when it seems to or attempts to deny linearity. Even Woolf, who knew the novel form differently, being one of the few people successful in remaking it (interestingly enough via a great deal of initial help from the critical eye and advice of her friend and rival, the short story writer Mansfield), depends on chronology. The wanderings in time of Mrs. Dalloway have to be held in the matrix of a single day. The flow of time and change in The Waves must still be held in a fundamentally consequential chronology between birth, death and birth in nine gestative sections.

Books themselves take time, more time than most of us are used to giving them. Books demand time. Sometimes they take and demand more time than we're ready or yet know how to grant them; they go at their own speed regardless of the cultural speed or slowness of their readers' zeitgeists. Plus, they're tangible pieces of time in our hands. We hold them for the time it takes to read them and we move through them and measure time passing by how far through them we've got, what the page-edge correlation (or percentage, if we're using a digital reader) between the beginning and the end is. Also, they travel with us, they accompany us through from our pasts into our futures, always with their present-tense ability, there as soon as they're opened, for words to act like the notes heard in music do, marking from word to word the present moment always in reference to what went before, what's on its way, in a phrase, a sentence, a paragraph, a section, a chapter.

We do treat books surprisingly lightly in contemporary culture. We'd never expect to understand a piece of music on one listen, but we tend to believe we've read a book after reading it just once. Books and music share more in terms of resonance than just a present-tense correlation of heard note to read word. Books need time to dawn on us, it takes time to understand what makes them, structurally, in thematic resonance, in afterthought, and always in correspondence with the books which came before them, because books are produced by books more than by writers; they're a result of all the books that went before them. Great books are adaptable; they alter with us as we alter in life, they renew themselves as we change and re-read them at different times in our lives. You can't step into the same story twice—or maybe it's that stories, books, art can't step into the same person twice, maybe it's that they allow for our mutability, are ready for us at all times, and maybe it's this adaptability, regardless of time, that makes them art, because real art (as opposed to more transient art, which is real too, just for less time) will hold us at all our different ages like it held all the people before us and will hold all the people after us, in an elasticity and with a generosity that allow for all our comings and goings. Because come then go we will, and in that order.

## 4: Haven't Found a Song Title for This Section Yet / something about linearity—maybe Time After Time or Everybody's Got to Learn Sometime (By the Korgis—check lyrics)

'It is never possible for a novelist to deny time inside the fabric of his novel,' Forster says, annoyingly. And, even more annoying, as Saramago points out early on in his 1986 novel, The Stone Raft (translated by Giovanni

Pontiero), the main problem with writing anything at all is that it's inevitably always linear—one word after another:

> Writing is extremely difficult, it is an enormous responsibility, you need only think of the exhausting work involved in setting out events in chronological order, first this one, then that, or, if considered more convenient to achieve the right effect, today's event placed before yesterday's episode, and other no less risky acrobatics, the past treated as if it were new, the present as a continuous process without any present or ending, but, however hard writers might try, there is one feat they cannot achieve, that is to put into writing, in the same tense, two events which have occurred simultaneously. Some believe the difficulty can be solved by dividing the page into two columns, side by side, but this strategy is ingenuous, because the one was written first and the other afterwards, without forgetting that the reader will have to read this one first and then the other one, or vice versa, the people who come off best are the opera singers, each with his or her own part to sing, three, four, five, six between tenors, basses, sopranos and baritones, all

singing different words, for example, the cynic mocking, the ingénue pleading, the gallant lover slow in coming to her aid, what interests the operagoer is the music, but the reader is not like this, he wants everything explained, syllable by syllable and one after the other.

Saramago's narrator is in a deep state of frustration here because in this novel, and germane to everything about this novel, he wants to describe, with the simultaneity with which he says they happen, three random happenings which all seem to have contributed to a crack appearing in the fabric of things, a piece of Europe breaking off from itself—the Iberian Peninsula—and floating away on its own terms. He wants to describe communally—in a uniting fashion, what you might call a harmony—a metaphor of terrible isolation. In the course of this novel, about whether men and women are islands or not, he examines both time's terrible political, historical, and environmental consequences (he does this in almost every novel he writes) and the things which really do seem to endure in the face of change between human beings—and not just human beings, but between humans and other species too.

Juan Pablo Villalobos's 2010 novel, Down the Rabbit Hole (translated by Rosalind Harvey), is narrated by a seven-year-old called Tochtli (or Rabbit), who is growing up surrounded by guns in a drug cartel in Mexico where the people his father has shot are literally thrown to the big cats they keep on the premises for eating the evidence:

> Books don't have anything in them about the present, only the past and the future. This is one of the biggest defects of books. Someone should invent a book that tells you what's happening at this moment, as you read. It must be harder to write that sort of book than the futuristic ones that predict the future. That's why they don't exist. And that's why I have to go and investigate reality.

This, in a novel about a child coming of age and learning by direct experience the meanings of beastly and manly, suggests a moral imperative to do with the meeting place of literature and time.

If the Roman historian Sallust could write, in his work on storytelling and myth, On the Gods and the World, summing up the paradox that comes about when fiction meets time, 'these things never happened, but are always,' what JG Ballard suggests all the centuries later is that the relationship between time and artful fictiveness has flayed itself inside out. In an introduction to his 1973 novel Crash, written in the 90s, he describes this upside-down world—suggests that now it's more a case of *these things happen, but never were.* We now 'live inside an enormous novel,' he writes, 'a world ruled by fictions of every kind—mass merchandising, advertising, politics conducted as a branch of advertising, the pre-empting of any original response to experience by the television screen.' Now we need our novelists to 'invent the reality.' His own novels tick like bombs.

But whether it involves a portrait locked away that changes and ages so that a man doesn't, or a little sweet cake that releases memory, or an arrow that flies backwards and undoes history, or a machine that can travel, or a ghost from the past, present, or future making a miser be generous, or a handmaid from the future, a Cromwell from the past: either way, anyway, it is always about now, both the now in which it is being written and the now in which it is being read. In Aspects of the Novel you can almost sense excitement beyond his customary charming diffidence when Forster writes about how Gertrude Stein 'has smashed up and pulverised her clock and scattered its fragments over the world like the limbs of Osiris, and she has done this not from naughtiness but from a noble motive: she has hoped to emancipate fiction from the tyranny of time.' It doesn't last; Forster's far too urbane for that kind of violence or primal rite. And such rites of modernism, though they still look alarmingly experimental to the mainstream eye, are old hat to us now a hundred years on, so post is a post is a post is a post. We're well past the end of the century when time, for the first time, curved, bent, slipped, flashforwarded and flashbacked yet still kept on rolling along. We know it all now, with our thoughts traveling at the speed of tweet, our 140 characters in search of a paragraph. We're post-history. We're post-mystery.

## 5: Please Mr. Post Man, Look and See: Remembrance of Things Post

The twentieth century was wedded to the remembrance of things past, with Proust making the act of remembrance an art of sensory timeslip in the first texts which would become A la Recherche du Temps Perdu in 1913 and with Joyce making an epic forever out of a single passing ordinary day with the serialization of the first chapters of Ulysses not long after.

Then at its center the twentieth century pivots on a vision like this one from Victor Klemperer, the Jewish academic and diarist whose career at the University of Dresden was interrupted in the 1930s by Nazi anti-Semitic laws, who lived out the war years on a knife edge, and who, having survived, just, writes the following in his diary on November 8, 1945, about sitting, not long after the defeat of Hitler's regime, listening to a talk on the radio (translated here by Martin Chalmers):

Radio Beromünster: Reddar (that's what the magic word sounded like), the English ray invention, which allowed them to see U-boats and guide air planes by wireless, and gave them victory at sea and in the air. Inserted in the talk a piece of a Hitler speech, the very piece I once myself heard standing outside the offices of the *Freiheitskampf*. And if the war lasts 3 years— we'll still have our say!—and if it lasts 4 years . . . and if 5, and if 6 . . . we will not capitulate! It was his voice! It was his voice, his agitated and inflammatory furi-ous shouting, I clearly recognised it again . . . And

with it applause and Nazi songs. A shatteringly present past . . . [To think] that this is past, and that its
presence can be restored to the present, always and at
every moment!

Almost as though he can't believe such repetition possible, Klemperer apes it here, repeats himself: 'It was his
voice! It was his voice . . .' But it's the phrase 'a shatteringly present past' that reveals a vandalism in this particular repetition. Old stories repeat themselves, but
always to new ends and always to this end: a renewal of
vision. What Klemperer—terribly—doesn't know is that
this past will still be playing in its endless numbing loop
on all our tv screens sixty years later in a new century.
The god technology, as Klemperer suggests sitting by the
radio speaker, is a Pandora of a box; it can make the invisible visible, do wonders, help win and stop foul wars,
and out of the same place comes the first shattering, then
numbing power to make history repeat until it becomes
banality (to use the word Hannah Arendt did to describe
Nazi evil).

Its knowing brings with it, like all knowledges, a twin
forgetfulness, and the most recent form this forgetful-

ness takes is made visible here in the following poem by
Jackie Kay, whose subject is a poet searching—doing an
online search—for an old poem of hers which happens to
be about another pivotal moment in time, the time when
one century turns into another. Its title is http://www
.google.co.uk/

> I thought I'd cut and pasted my poem about the year 1999
> but when I pressed paste all that came up was
>
> > http://www.google.co.uk/
>
> so I decided to look up Mahler symphony no 7 in Wikipedia
> but when I went on line Wikipedia was blacked out for 24 hours
> and they wanted me to twitter my support
>
> And when I hit google a message said google isn't your default
>
> > browser
>
> which made me feel worried though I don't understand why
> and my poem had vanished: it was a poem about my
>
> > grandmother
>
> who was the wife of a miner twice buried alive in the pit,
> who survived who came back up into the air in Fife.
> It's a worry if when you go to paste your poem to send to your
>
> > friend

your poem has been replaced by http://www.google.co.uk/

If you can't import your poem or attach your poem

will it be enough to be attached to your poem, to the memory of it

now that it has gone, vanished into cyber space.


Cyber space has no face, not like the face of my grandmother.

Every line of this is true and as I was writing this

even this disappeared for a second and a dashboard appeared

with a clock, a calculator and an icon of safari.

The clock told me it is 3 o'clock in Amsterdam.


Kay's poem about a lost poem is all about surface and depth. It asks about a disappearing truth, a lost attachment to the past, a lost attachment to the process of art. It makes visible, instead, a blocked or diverted set of connections. It asks what, in this case, attachment actually means, when it (and we?) can so easily be disappeared, when histories of survival and stratification can so simply vanish in front of our eyes. Its last stanza is a driverless car, a place where the present is slippery, can't be trusted; the 'true' lines—precariously there one minute, gone the next—echo the lost lines of the human face, exchanged not just for the face of a clock but a clock that tells an irrelevant time.

\*

"Tis down in yonder garden green,
Love, where we used to walk,
The finest flower that ere was seen
Is withered to a stalk.
'The stalk is withered dry, my love,
So will our hearts decay;
So make yourself content, my love,
Till God calls you away.'

I'd been at a loss so I'd gone and stood in the study, which I only ever did when I felt the very worst. The desk was piled up with the talks you'd been supposed to give at that university. On the top was the one about time. I'd picked the first page up (suncurled, dried, a bit faded), I'd glanced at it and at the still quite pristine page below it and I'd laughed when I'd seen Walter Benjamin's name, because, much like my brother used to shout when we were kids in the back of the car and we were driving south, Ten points to the first person who can see the Forth Road Bridge, or my father when he was teaching me to drive, Ten points if you can hit that woman crossing the road, what you used to say when you'd make me come with you to those boring conferences was, Ten points to the first person who hears someone say the words Walter Benjamin.

My own job was trees; I knew about how they prepare themselves for winter way back in the summer, how they ready themselves in the winter for the fruiting months. Unlike flowers which die right down every year and have to start all over again, break the surface again, trees can keep going from where they left off. I knew about small willow moths, clearwings, leopard moths, buff-tip moths, and goat moths and exactly what kinds of willow they preferred.

Ten points to the first person to see someone back from the dead. There was an explanation for the stain where the tea had sunk into the floorboards. I'd done it myself, obviously. But I had to congratulate my imagination, for you were very like you. Though I'd never have imagined the imagination could be so good with smell; you smelt quite strong for something or someone imaginary. Either way, you'd come back, and it was about time.

But if I went to bed and went to sleep, would you still be here when I woke up?

Tell me where you've been, I'd said to you earlier. What's it like? And don't just say 'what's *been*, again?'

Come on. You used to know all the words. You knew more words than anyone. Tell me.

Your black eyes gleamed like cut coals, animal eyes. You raised your arm and hit the wall next to the bookcase.

Four, you said.

You mean the wall? I said. You mean four walls? Like a prison?

You shook your head. I could almost hear you thinking. It was like the noise a broken tree makes when its broken part, after lightning has hit and split it, is too heavy for the rest of the tree, is about to split right off and fall. With great effort, you spoke. You pointed first at one wall then another.

Dark. Dark. Dark. But one is light.

Three dark walls and one light wall? I said.

You tapped the coffee table with your hand.

Again? you said.

It's a table, I said.

Yes, a table, and people, food, a woman, hair, it's what is it? Light, bright hair.

There's a woman there? I said. With bright hair? What woman? Who? Do you know her?

And a man, next to the woman, you said.

Oh, right, I said. Is he *with* the woman? Or is the woman something to do with you?

—he's got, it's wood, with, what is it, again? String? Hand. A man, and the wood with the string, in his hand, you know. Epomony.

He what? I said.

Epomony, you said. Epomony.

Oh, the imagination was fantastic: mine didn't just make up some place you'd been, it even made up words whose meanings I didn't know—which was exactly what it had been like, to live with you. In fact when I went through and tried to look up that word in the dictionary I couldn't find a word like it. So the imagination was even more amazing than I'd given it credit for. Lying in bed now, for instance, with you next to me with all your clothes still on, I could actually feel what felt like real grit and dust all along the underside of my left thigh.

D'you think you could take the mug out of your pocket? I said. It's poking into my hip bone there and it's actually quite sore.

Mud, you said.

Mug, I said.

Mud, you said again. Then you said the word: fog. Then the word: town.

Where? I said. Where you were?

Oliver, you said. Twist.

How'd you know I'm reading Oliver Twist? I was about to say. But you'd begun to snore.

If only I'd reimagined you without your snoring. But then it wouldn't have been true, would it? It wouldn't have been you.

I lay there beside you, beside myself in the dust and grit of you, because though you were gone you were here, and what would happen next? Whatever happened, I'd let it, because it knows us inside out, the imagination. It knows us better than we know ourselves. It couldn't have been more timely. It knows the time of day all right.

# On form

I placed a jar in Tennessee
because I could not stop for death
to see a world in a grain of sand
where Alph, the sacred river, ran.

Nobody heard him, the dead man
alone and palely loitering,
rage, rage against the dying of
the golden apples of the sun.

You stand at the blackboard, daddy.
Let the traffic policemen wear black cotton gloves.
And for that minute a blackbird sang.
What will survive of us is love.

It would maybe have been better if you could have
come back from the dead a bit differently. I mean if
you could have come back as an array of different yous,
like anyone with the originality you had when you

were alive should naturally have done; for instance if you'd come back as a dog, a mythical sort of one, one that could speak and would even occasionally do my bidding, occasionally sit at the table with me and converse while we ate our dinner, or if you'd come back as a small star, or a wing or a tongue of flame hovering above my head whenever I went anywhere, or a mystic vision of, I don't know, an ibis, or a waterfall which would just suddenly appear, or a flowering bush or an angel or a devil or a rain of coins, a puff of mist with a big paw for a hand like in the Italian picture of the woman being held in an embrace by nothing but a gray-black raincloud.

Because when I think about what it was like to live with you, it was like all these things. It was like living in a poem or a picture, a story, a piece of music, when I think of it now. It was wonderful.

Not that I wasn't glad you were back, coming and going like you did over the weeks, the same you only slightly more ragged-looking every time, and every time coming in like I wasn't even there and going straight over and sitting at the study desk, pulling your hair out over those talks you had been going to give about books and art. I never saw you doing any actual writing, I only ever saw you pulling your hair out.

You'll be bald soon if you keep doing that, I said.

Like the nodding De Chirico heads in Sylvia Plath's The Disquieting Muses, you said from your seat at the desk.

If you say so, I said, whatever they are when they're at home.

It's a poem, you said, about a frightening childhood vision which partly inspires a child to be an artist and partly leaves her no option but to be it. I should write about Plath in this talk on form. She's someone who works so hard to master form in her earlier poems that in the later poems she finds a kind of formal liberation and can do anything she likes.

Right, I said. Uh huh.

It was like you had no idea you were dead.

It's *because* of the tightness of stanza, you were saying, and the syllabic patterning in her early poems, poems like Black Rook in Rainy Weather, that when she gets to the final work, the poems in Ariel, she *can* fly completely free-form. But only because she's understood it in the first place. It's like the tightness of form in the early poet releases the openness of form in the later.

Yeah, and she lived a jolly life, didn't she, happy and fulfilled and so on, I said.

You turned your black eyes and your blackening nose on me and you sighed.

I've told you a hundred times, the *life* is nothing to *do* with it, you said. The *life* is the *least* of it.

You were back on form yourself. You could speak again without having to stop and wonder what words meant, though you were a bit nasal-sounding now; you were sounding more and more alarmingly like your old self with each visit home, and you were staying longer with me each time, though your actual nose now was almost gone, was sort of hollow, and the smell you sent ahead of yourself was so much worse than the clean earthy smell you'd first had when you came back that when I came home from work and walked up our street now I'd always know several houses away if you were there or not, and also there'd been some notes through the letterbox from next door, about drains, and I tried not to mind that every time you left again more things from the house would have gone missing: my watch, almost all the pens, the remotes for both the tv and the dvd (which meant I couldn't actually switch them on), the little onyx owl off the mantelpiece, the red pair of pliers, the recharger for the electric toothbrush, the tweezers, even once a whole table lamp went; and I tried not to mind that you seemed more interested, when you did come here, in spending time poring over those old unfinished talks you never even gave at a university than in me, since of course it was because of me, not them, you were coming back here at all, wasn't it?

But if anything was imperfect about you it was my own doing. As you'd always said, the imagination can do anything. If only mine was half as original as yours had been I'd have been *able* to imagine you odorless, sitting up at the table with me like that good talking dog or hovering starlike above me wherever I went, through the supermarkets and train stations of life. But no, I couldn't even imagine you a good permanent nose. I didn't even have the imaginative grace to be able to do that. And there seemed nothing I could do to change it: though I tried to imagine it differently it always ended up the same every time you came home, through the door, up the stairs and straight into the study to pull out more of your hair over some old computer printouts.

At the moment the one that was preoccupying you was the one called On Form.

I wasn't really sure, to be honest, what form meant. I asked Sandra, at work. It's a thing you fill in, she said.

Ha, I said, because little did she know that right at that moment I was sitting there experimenting with some stiff paper, curving it into a cone shape for filling the place your nose had been, I was thinking that paper was better than wood, not too heavy and very easily replaceable and re-shape-able. I had noticed that you were having trouble, with no place on your face now to balance your glasses.

Yeah but Sandra, I said. What's the form for if a dead person comes back from the dead and hangs out with you? What would you do if that happened to you? Ha ha, Sandra said, who's been watching too many horror movies. Then she looked concerned and said: Are you all right sweetheart? No, I'm fine, I said. Well, we all thought you were on better form than you'd been, she said, we're all glad about that, you've had a rough time. But you're looking a bit pale these days again, I was wondering if things were okay at home. No, but really, I said, what if someone, what would you do with them? Sandra looked at me then looked hard at her computer screen. If it happened to me, she said not looking up from the screen, I'd tell someone. I am, I'm telling you, I said. I mean, I'd go and see a doctor, she said. That's what I'd do if I were you.

She sent me out to check ten sycamores at the backs of some houses in Romsey to see whether there was a root problem when it came to the sewers (the sycamores were fine, though a leylandii clump was too close to the houses by far) and by the time I got back to work she'd sent me an email saying I'd been assigned next week off, on half-pay—in October, which is one of our busiest times.

I looked up hotels in Brighton. We'd always liked going to Brighton. I booked one we'd stayed in before. I walked home. You were home already; I could tell.

I've booked a holiday, I said. Want to come? We need some fresh air, you and me. But if you don't want to, that's okay. If you'd rather stay here with your work, I mean.

You didn't hear me. You were busy working. I watched hair waft down lightly through the air in the bright of the anglepoise.

Two days later, two days into the holiday, two days of waking at 5 am and knowing there was nothing to have to get up for, two days away from the work structure hanging around a hotel room by myself with you, and I was losing the will to live.

On our first day I'd wandered round the shops near the hotel. When I got back I found you'd clearly been right behind me and had lifted a couple of books from the charity bookshop whose stock I'd had a passing look at. I began to worry. You were a figment of my imagination. That meant I must have taken those things.

Did you just take those? Without paying? I said.

You held up one of the hotel coffee mugs. Then you let it drop. It hit a bit of floor that wasn't carpeted and broke into splintery pieces.

You can't do that kind of thing, I said, not here.

You picked up one of the pieces and examined it as closely as you'd examined the complete mug a moment ago.

Beautiful, you said.

You can't just break things, I said. It's not done. And you can't just take things. It's okay to take things from *home*. But not from shops.

You opened one of the books, a small old kind of book

with a bright yellow cover, drawings of birds all over it. It was called Birds at Sight: How to Know Them.

*Lesser spotted woodpecker. The nest is a hole in a tree,* you said. *Jay. The nest of sticks and grass is in a bush or tree. Magpie. The domed nest with entrance at the side is built of sticks and mud in a tree or bush. Linnet. The nest of rootlets, grass, wool and hair is in a gorse bush or similar place. Chaffinch. The mossy nest with soft lining is one of the prettiest, and may be in a bush, hedge or tree.*

Actually it's not really all right to keep taking things from home either, I said.

*The wonderful bottle-shaped mud nest is under the eaves of a building,* you read. *All the mud is brought in the birds' bills. The nest is in a crevice in a wall or tree or on a beam in the roof of a building.*

I don't mind so much the pens and stuff, I said. But there are some things I need you not to take.

*The cock sparrow, courting, will display his throat and droop his wings,* you said. *He brings and tears yellow flowers. The male whitethroat, courting, will bring the female a piece of grass.*

The car key, I said. And my bank cards. The car key cost £260 to replace. I can't drive the car without it. And

it's very annoying and inconvenient to have to keep changing my bank cards.

*Hopping birds, such as the sparrows, blackbirds,*
*thrushes and other finches leave their footprints in pairs,*
*side by side. Walking or running birds, like the wagtail*
*and the starling, leave a line of alternate impressions,*
*similar in form to human tracks.*

Well, obviously, I said.

You went on reading out stuff at me about the differ-
ences between footprints left by ducks and gulls.

I'm going out, I said. Don't come too.

I went for a walk at the shore. It was nice to be by
myself. Then I realized I was looking at the tracks birds
had left, watching for what gulls' tracks looked like, and
I got annoyed at myself and at you. Then I felt guilty for
enjoying being by myself.

It started to rain. I ducked into one of the shop spaces
under the walkway. It was an amusement arcade full of
old machines, the kind from the first few decades of the
last century. I gave the man in the booth a pound and he
gave me ten old pennies in exchange; then I halfheart-
edly wound my way two-thirds through a lady lifting her
skirts in a What the Butler Saw machine, showing her
thighs higher and higher in a flicketing wad of old photo-

graphs whose paper edges, as they shifted from still to motion to still again, were so softened and dirty, so like old worthless currency, that I felt sorry for the white-thighed lady, then for all the people who'd ever put their eyes to this eyeslot and watched her, then finally for myself, which I continued to feel, wandering round this arcade. Until, that is, I found the Super Steer-a-Ball.

The Super Steer-a-Ball was a big square machine painted bright red with a sloping metal countryside painted onto it and a steering wheel stuck on the front. I put a penny in and a steel ball about the size of a child-hood gobstopper appeared through a hole at the top. The ball had to be guided down a maze of sloping paths between panels enameled with summer trees, avoiding dead ends and hidden slopes, until it reached two holes and disappeared into the blackness down one of them. The holes were rusty, very roughly cut in the metal. One hole had the word HOME written next to it in red. The other had the word LOST.

I put all the cash I had and all the change in my pockets into this machine, because every time I put the penny in, no matter what I did, the ball went down the hole marked LOST. They were just holes, the holes, cut in the metal. They were exactly the same as each other. But one was called HOME and one was called LOST, so I kept on putting my penny in and trying to get the ball into the one marked HOME. It was terrible, the fact that it kept going down the one marked LOST.

I had started the walk with sixty pounds in my wallet. I went to the booth now with my last five-pound note.

The Super Steer-a-Ball is impossible, I said to the man in the booth.

Oh no it's not, he said.

Oh yes it is, I said. It can't be done.

Oh yes it can, he said.

He took an old penny for himself off one of the stacks of coins and opened the door to the booth, came out, stood in front of the machine, put his penny in and angled the steering wheel acutely as the ball came down through the pretty trees and went straight down the hole marked LOST.

Aw, the man said. I can usually. Wait a minute.

I gave him one of my pennies. He put it in, the ball came down the English lanes and went straight down the hole marked LOST.

I'd have liked another couple of tries myself, but I couldn't get him off the game. So I served the small queue of people for him who were waiting for change. When I left the arcade he was still bracing his own weight against the weight of the machine.

Aw! he was saying. Then: Wait. Then: Aw no.

I came back to our hotel, which was quite a posh one. I moved through Reception as quickly as I could because some people there were making a complaint to the management about drains. I came upstairs, along the corridor and into our room. You were still sitting exactly where you'd been, as if I'd never left. You were reading the other book you'd stolen from the charity shop, a book about the ways insects, birds, and bigger creatures made homes for themselves out of whatever they had to hand. *Compare this*, I read over your shoulder, *with the saliva nest constructed by Asian cave swiftlets. Made of solidified spit, the secretion's function is to form a bracket nest for attachment to a cave wall. Other species, like the glossy swiftlet, differ in that they use their saliva to stick plant materials together.*

There was a photograph of a crusted, waxy-looking bird hammock, a paragraph about bird's nest soup and a further description of an Australian caterpillar that used its own feces to make a little hut.

I went and lay on the bed and I tried my hardest, I imagined you putting the book down and coming and lying beside me there on the bed.

It worked. You put the book down. You came over. You lay down, almost obediently.

I looked into your black eyes.

Home. Lost.

Tell me some more, I said, about the place you go, the place you are when you're not with me. The place with the woman with the bright hair in it.

Oh, you said. Okay. Well. There's three dark walls and one wall covered with light. On this wall there's a woman, a girl, with bright hair. And sometimes she's all colorful and sometimes there's no color but her hair is bright every time. And she lives in a village on an island, and there's an old sea captain in the same village, only he's gone mad now that he's been on land for so long, and she goes to the docks with him and they stand and look out over the sea and imagine all the places they could go, they shout the names of all the places at the sea and the sky.

Yes, I said.

I closed my eyes and listened.

And then she's very poor, living in a poor part of the city, and she can't keep a job because every place she takes one the boss makes a pass at her because she's so pretty, so she decides she'll emigrate, and a kind neighbor tells her about his friend, a man who sends ships all over the world, he says this man will help her, and she goes to see him, the man, and he takes a liking to her, and after she's left his office he finds she's dropped her purse. He looks inside it and there's almost nothing, a few small notes, a few coins. In a little while he's going to take a large note out of his own wallet and fold it into the purse and give the purse back to her without her knowing he's done this. Meanwhile she's on a bus and has just looked in her bag and can't find her purse, and the conductor is standing over her about to ask for the money for her ticket.

Then what? I said.

Then it's in color and she's stowed away on a boat to be near her true love, who's a sailor, a cadet, and she's hiding in a lifeboat under the canvas covers waiting for the chance to come out and some sailors come and stand round the lifeboat, they're all eating bread and cheese. And one of them asks another one to play a tune on his

harmonica, so he puts his bread and cheese on the cover
of the lifeboat and plays a tune, and while they're all listening to him, inside under the lifeboat cover she sees the
shadow of the food and licks her lips and her hand sneaks
out and takes the cheese and the bread. The man finishes
playing the tune and he looks for his bread and cheese,
it's gone, and he thinks it was a trick by the other sailors,
getting him to play a tune so they could take his sand-
wich, and a squabble breaks out, but inside the boat the
girl eats the bread and the cheese with a look of total happiness on her face.

Through all these weeks you'd been back, whenever I'd asked you about the other place you'd been,
you'd told me little pieces of story like these, always
about this hungry, bright-headed girl. Then you'd say
words I'd never heard of, words that didn't really sound
like they were words. It was good, that things didn't
have to mean. It was a relief. It was strangely intimate,
too, you speaking to me and me having no idea what you
were saying.

Guide a ruckus, you said now. Trav a brose. Spoo yattacky. Clot so. Scoofy.

Tell me what else happens, I said. Say more things
like that.

\*

To stay anxiety I engrave this gold,

Shaping an amulet whose edges hold

A little space of order: where I find,

Suffused with light, a dwelling for the mind.


(CLIVE WILMER, The Goldsmith)


## 1: Putting the For in Form

In the beginning was the word, and the word was what made the difference between form and formlessness, which isn't to suggest that the relationship between form and formlessness isn't a kind of dialogue too, or that formlessness had no words, just to suggest that this particular word for some reason made a difference between them—one that started things.

'God, or some such artist as resourceful, / Began to sort it out. / Land here, sky there, / And sea there' is how Ovid, metamorphosing into Ted Hughes, saw the start of all things. Before that? 'Everything fluid or vapor, form formless. / Each thing hostile / To every other thing.' Not that fluid or vapor isn't form too; it's the hostility that Hughes highlights: 'at every point / Hot fought cold, moist dry, soft hard, and the weightless / Resisted weight.' Until, that is, God, or some such artist, starts throwing weight around. Form, from the Latin *forma*, meaning shape. Shape, a mold; something that holds or shapes; a species or kind; a pattern or type; a way of being; order, regularity, system. It once meant beauty but now that particular meaning's obsolete. It means style and arrangement, structural unity in music, literature, painting, etc.; ceremony; behavior; condition of fitness or efficiency. It means the inherent nature of an object, that in which the essence of a thing consists. It means a long seat, or a bench, or a school class, and also the shape a hare makes in the grass with its body for a bed. It's versatile. It holds us, it molds us, it identifies us, it shows us how to be, it gives us a blueprint in life and art, it's about essentiality, and several of us can sit on it at once. It can mean a criminal record and it can mean correctness of procedure, both at once. Form can be right and it can be wrong. This is Graham Greene on Shakespeare's felicity of form even in the slightest of phrases, in a throwaway moment from Troilus and Cressida: '"Think, we had mothers," Troilus's bitter outburst is not poetry in any usually accepted meaning of the word—it is simply the right phrase at the right moment, a mathematical accuracy . . . in a balance sensitive to the fraction of a milligram.'

And this is Thom Gunn, talking of Yvor Winters, on the uses of the poetic form: 'poetry was an instrument for exploring the truth of things, as far as human beings can explore it, and it can do so with a greater verbal exactitude than prose can manage.'

Why? Why can't prose 'manage' this 'greater verbal exactitude'? Simply because we don't allocate to prose the lingual attention, the aura, the essentiality, that we do to poetry? Because we *want* the forms to be different?

Form is a matter of clear rules *and* unspoken understandings, then. It's a matter of need and expectation. It's also a matter of breaking rules, of dialogue, crossover between forms. Through such dialogue and argument, form, the shaper and molder, acts like the other thing called mold, endlessly breeding forms from forms.

Not marble nor the gilded monuments
of princes shall outlive this powerful rhyme,
But you shall shine more bright in these contents
Than unswept stone besmeared with sluttish time.
When wasteful war shall statues overturn,

And broils root out the work of masonry,

Nor Mars his sword, nor war's quick fire shall burn

The living record of your memory.

Gainst death and all oblivious enmity

Shall you pace forth, your praise shall still find room

Even in the eyes of all posterity

That wear this world out to the ending doom.

So, till the judgement that yourself arise,

You live in this, and dwell in lovers' eyes.

The power of the artform is stronger than stone, the poet says, and chooses the sonnet, a form concerned with argument and persuasion, to say so. This sonnet, he says, will last longer than any gravestone—*and* you'll be made shinier, brighter, by it. In this form it will—and therefore you will—avoid destruction by war, history, time generally; it'll even keep you alive after death; in fact it'll form a place for you to live, not die, where you'll be seen in the eyes of and the context of this love right to the end of time.

But there's always another story, there's always another way to see the shape of things: up against Shakespeare's overweening gorgeous sweet arrogant protective and still very well functioning preservative form, here's a jarring anecdote from Wallace Stevens:

I placed a jar in Tennessee,
And round it was, upon a hill.
It made the slovenly wilderness
Surround that hill.

The wilderness rose up to it,
And sprawled around, no longer wild.
The jar was round upon the ground
And tall and of a port in air.

It took dominion everywhere.
The jar was gray and bare.
It did not give of bird or bush,
Like nothing else in Tennessee.

The jar, the made thing, the not-natural thing, orders the reality round it, subtracts its wildness, its will; this plain repetitive form in its too-roundedness leaves the world, in which it becomes the central form, 'sprawling'—it masters 'everywhere'—and at the same time the poem pushes back at and away from its own formal urge, it argues with itself, refuses to do quite what the form should, syllabically and in terms of our expectations of rhyme. Where's the rhyme for bush? There isn't one. Or for wilderness.

The only thing that rhymes with Tennessee is Tennessee; same for hill. Rhyme, in this poem, connects air and everywhere to the word bare.

There'll always be a dialogue, an argument, between aesthetic form and reality, between form and its content, between seminality, art, fruitfulness, and life. There'll always be a seminal argument between forms—that's how forms produce themselves, out of a meeting of opposites, of different things; out of form encountering form. Put two poems together and they'll make a third:

Not Marble: a Reconstruction

A Sqezy bottle in Tennessee,
if you want permanence, will press
a dozen jars into the wilderness.
It's bright, misspelt, unpronounceably
itself. No one loves you! I guess
there's *amour propre* in a detergent not to be
called sluttish. Vulgarity
dogs marble, gildings; monuments are a mess.
*Exegi* this, *exegi* that. Let's say
I am in love, crushed under the weight
of it or elated under the hush of it.

Let's not just say. I actually am.
Hordes, posterities, judges vainly cram
the space my love and I left yesterday.


Litter-ature! Litter is even brighter than, more powerful than, more enduring than art, and 'if you want permanence,' Edwin Morgan says in this 1987 poem, it'll
last. But the poem, absolutely about contemporary forms,
unites Stevens and Shakespeare then digs back through
the landfill past them both to Shakespeare's original
source for Sonnet 55, Horace's Odes: exegi monumentum
aere perennius: I have raised a monument more permanent than bronze. So what? says Morgan, intent on pushing past the gesture, the 'just saying' of words: 'Let's not
just say. I actually am.' Morgan revels in the space, the
not-marble, the nothing-but-air left by the lovers, into
which the future can rush, fill if it likes, because this
form, made from nothing-but-air, in being so permeable,
is impermeable, the lovers being gone. And the loveliness
of the rhyming somersault in Morgan's sonnet, cr*ush*ed
under the w*eight* of it or el*ate*d under the *hush* of it,
bowls him over and we're back to lightness versus weight
again, the relationships between weight, lightness of
touch, space, and air.

It's about the connecting force from form to form. It's the toe bone connecting to the shoulder bone. It's the bacterial kick of life force, something growing out of nothing, forming itself out of something else. Form never stops. And form is always environmental. Like a people's songs will tell you about the heart and the aspirations of that people, like their language and their use of it will tell you what their concerns are, material and metaphysical, their artforms will tell you everything about where they live and the shape they're in.

For those in the business of making aesthetic forms, the god-business, the business of calibration, the questions and complications of aesthetic presence and absence, instinct and craft, are complex ones riddled with hubris, humility, hope, respect. 'It will be a great miracle to make a painted man a real one,' as Michelangelo (translated by Christopher Ryan) wrote in one of his poems; there's a story about him hitting one of his just-finished statues and yelling, furious, 'Speak, why don't you?' To cut this urge down to size, here's the start of another of his sonnets: 'The greatest artist does not have any concept which a single piece of marble does not itself contain within its excess, though only a hand that obeys the intellect can discover it.' Woolf suggested some similar crucial understanding between thought, essence, reality, and form when she wrote about 'the born writer's gift of being in touch with the thing itself and not with the outer husks of words.' Let's not just say. I actually am.

We make form and form makes us. Form can gladden us, tease and worry and madden us, like it does in Ciaran Carson's description of the art of storytelling, near the beginning of his 1999 work, Fishing for Amber:

Or sometimes, plagued by his children for yet another story, my father would appear to yield, and begin, It was a stormy night in the Bay of Biscay, and the Captain and his sailors were seated around the fire. Suddenly, one of the sailors said, Tell us a story, Captain. And the Captain began, It was a stormy night in the Bay of Biscay, and the Captain and his sailors were seated around the fire. Suddenly, one of the sailors said, Tell us a story, Captain. And the Captain began, It was a stormy night in the Bay of Biscay, and the Captain and his sailors were seated around the fire. Suddenly, one of the sailors said—

Carson is always asking questions of form, with everything he writes. His novels are collections of stories; his

realities are all fiction-driven, his fictions and his poetry
are as attached to reality and politics as it's possible for
anything to be. His forms are creative fusions that stir up
the possibilities of form. Here it's as if he's found the essence of form itself—it can generate dimensionality out
of nothing, out of repetition, out of fusion, even out of its
own barrenness like Stevens's jarring jar. It sorts the
shape from the shapeless—not that the shapeless doesn't
have form too, it does, because nothing doesn't. Even
formlessness has form.

And it suggests this truth about the place where aesthetic form meets the human mind. For even if we were
to find ourselves homeless, in a strange land, with nothing of ourselves left—say we lost everything—we'd still
have another kind of home, in aesthetic form itself, in the
familiarity, the unchanging assurance that a known
rhythm, a recognized line, the familiar shape of a story, a
tune, a line or phrase or sentence gives us every time,
even long after we've forgotten we even know it. I placed
a jar in Tennessee. Once we know it, we'll never not know
it. Rough winds do shake the darling buds of May. They
always will. Rhythm itself is a kind of form and, regardless of whether it's poetry or prose, it becomes a kind of
dwelling place for us.

In its apparent fixity, form is all about change. In its fixity, form is all about the relationship of change to continuance, even when the continuance is itself precarious—here, for instance, this fragility *and* its opposite sureness are evident in the form, the diminishing line-length, and the thematic preoccupation of Wisława Szymborska's six-line poem (translated by Cavanagh and Bara'nczak), called, simply, Vermeer:

> So long as that woman from the Rijksmuseum
> in painted quiet and concentration
> keeps pouring milk day after day
> from the pitcher to the bowl
> the World hasn't earned
> the world's end.

## 2: Putting the Form in Transformation

These headings of yours for the different sections of your talks moved me. They were very like you. They were corny, a bit tentative, a bit bullish; they were kind of awful and it was as if they knew this about themselves and were vulnerable to it. The fact that you had capital-

ized the words the and in, in Putting The Form In Transformation, made me feel both vulnerable for you and
proud of you.

I was reading your On Form talk: well, I was glancing
at its start. One of us had brought it to Brighton with us:
me, of course. You, lying next to me now in your dark
sleeping form, didn't exist, weren't there. The pages of
On Form had been there, though, under my copy of Oliver Twist and the stolen books from the charity shop,
next to the hotel bedside light on my side of the bed when
I switched it on. 4:30 am and I was awake: again, much
like life used to be, me waking in the middle of the night
to you angsting about something you hadn't finished.
Calm down, I said once. Go and do a line of Shakespeare.
I actually made you laugh with that. I think you even put
it into one of your lectures. Maybe it was in this one.

I flicked the pages. My eye caught on the word heart.
It was in a quote: *Alas, the heart is not a metaphor—or
not only a metaphor.* That was good. I liked that. That
was true. It was someone called Elizabeth Hardwick,
from page 91 of a book that had the word Sleepless in the
title. When I was a child and we'd been given an American reading system at school for learning grammar, a system where you were assigned a color to let you know your

place in the class, i.e., the people doing Orange were near the bottom and were doing the easiest level and the people doing Aqua, Silver, and Gold were right up at the top doing the most difficult (as if to make hierarchy more bearable—as if we didn't know exactly what it meant, to be Orange), the teacher gave us the plasticized sheets to work from without ever telling us anything out loud about them, which meant that for a couple of years I thought that metaphor was pronounced with the stress on the a, like the word metabolism, and that the word simile was pronounced to rhyme with smile.

There were always questions on the backs of the plasticized sheets, I remember, about similes and metaphors in the extracts printed on the fronts of them. I never knew I'd grow up to marry someone whose stock-in-trade would be simile and metaphor. I never knew I'd grow up to marry anyone.

Simile, though your heart is breaking. It was Charlie Chaplin who wrote that tune, I remembered. Then the moment in Modern Times where he plays a workman who gets stuck in the mechanics of the machine he works on came into my head—not the moment of his being stuck in there, but the moment when, after he's freed himself from the machine, it's as if he's broken free from himself too; he does a dance with two spanners held up to his head like antlers, like he's gone lust-mad and being freed from the machine has changed him into a mad mythical creature, a faun, a Pan, like in classical paintings.

So, was metaphor about form, and was simile? How? I glanced down the page. *The copula of metaphor.* That sounded interesting. It sounded sexy. Funny to think: I'd known that simile involved like, but I hadn't ever thought that metaphor might involve love. *My heart is like a singing bird . . . My heart is like an apple-tree . . . Because my love is come to me.* So simile maybe involved love too. Well, he or she was lucky, having a heart like an apple tree. Even a broken apple tree will know what to do, with a bit of help, to right itself and have its fruit again. Even after the worst storm damage, a tree, so long as there's some green in the break, can be healed and mended and carry on growing. Unless, that is, the heart was like one of the literally thousands of kinds of apple tree that have disappeared from the British Isles in reasonably recent history because of the way the supermarkets only really like to sell about five kinds of apple.

That would be something: to have a heart whose tree produced a fruit that had otherwise died out. I saw that there was a lot about trees in this section. I wondered if,

when you'd been writing it—with me in the next room
probably reading the paper or watching the news, anyway
with no idea you were writing these exact words I was
reading now—if when you'd got to this bit about trees
you'd thought at all about me and my daily job, my own
stock-in-trade. There was a description here of a woman
who turns into a tree when she doesn't want to sleep with
a god, and another of an ancient couple who get turned
into trees so that they'll always be together, they'll never
have to die. That was beautiful. It was from Ovid. I would
find that Ovid book when I got home and read it. It would
be the book I'd read next, after I'd finished Oliver Twist.
If I ever finished Oliver Twist.

I started reading the bit about Ezra Pound. I was
amazed, actually, to find Ezra Pound in your talk, because I remembered you telling me that he was an anti-
Semitic old fascist and had been put in a cage for it. But
here he was: there was a quote from a poem of his: *I stood
still and was a tree amid the wood, / Knowing the truth
of things unseen before*, and then there was a long quote:

> The first myths arose when a man walked sheer into
> 'nonsense,' that is to say, when some very vivid and
> undeniable adventure befell him, and he told some-

one else who called him a liar. Thereupon, after bitter experience, perceiving that no one could understand what he meant when he said that he 'turned into a tree,' he made a myth—a work of art that is—an impersonal and objective story woven out of his own emotion, as the nearest equation that he was capable of putting into words. That story, perhaps, then gave rise to a weaker copy of his emotion in others.

Then there were a few lines scribbled out, I couldn't read them, then legible again more of your own words: *suggests what metaphor might be for, if 'warmth's the very stuff of poesy,' and takes the form of a prayer whose closing lines are:*

Oh, God, make small
The old star-eaten blanket of the sky,
That I may fold it round me and in comfort lie.

A writer like Flaubert (you continued), on the other hand, seems keen precisely to avoid the personalizing comforts of metaphor. One of the most recent translators of Madame Bovary, Lydia Davis, notes: 'In keeping with his plain, almost clinical approach to the material, he schooled himself to be very sparing with his metaphors. Often enough, in his intensive revising, the version he cut was more lyrical than the one he let stand.' In Madame Bovary, a novel very much about the responsibilities of literature, Flaubert goes out of his way to literalize metaphor when he uses it:

> Love, she believed, must come suddenly, with great thunderclaps and bolts of lightning,—a hurricane from heaven that drops down on your life, overturns it, tears away your will like a leaf, and carries your whole heart off with it into the abyss. She did not know that the rain forms lakes on the terraces of houses when the drainpipes are blocked, and thus she would have lived on feeling quite safe, had she not suddenly discovered a crack in the wall.

Metaphor has, he suggests, mundane literal consequence. And what might be called his most noted, most famous simile in Madame Bovary, which comes when Rodolphe, the seducer, is weighing up the worth of his affair with Emma, suggests Flaubert's vision of the shortchanging that happens when forms become fixed or clichéd; his underlying suggestion is that form must reinvent itself if it is to be meaningful or to continue being able to mean:

He had heard these things said to him so often that for him there was nothing original about them. Emma was like all other mistresses; and the charm of novelty, slipping off gradually like a piece of clothing, revealed in its nakedness the eternal monotony of passion, which always assumes the same forms and uses the same language. He could not perceive—this man of such broad experience—the difference in feelings that might underlie similarities of expression. Because licentious or venal lips had murmured the same words to him, he had little faith in their truthfulness; one had to discount, he thought, exaggerated speeches that concealed mediocre affections; as if the fullness of the soul did not sometimes overflow in the emptiest of metaphors, since none of us can ever express the exact measure of our needs, or our ideas, or our sorrows, and human speech is like a cracked kettle on which we beat out tunes for bears to dance to, when we long to move the stars to pity.

On this subject of literal consequence, a form of Flaubert's formal mistrust—his concern about language's metaphoric metamorph for good or ill—occurs in the writing of a man who remade the novel entirely, W. G. Sebald. In his last work, Austerlitz (translated here by Anthea Bell)—and arguably his most novel-like novel, while simultaneously a work intensely uneasy with notions of fiction and with itself as a fiction—in its most virtuosic, most tortuous, darkest passage, an eleven-page-long single sentence about the concentration camp Theresienstadt and about relentless connectivity, paralleled here in both language and industrialized mass murder, he uses simile *only once*, to describe prisoners who've been made to stand in ranked rows and in severe winter weather for many hours, 'bowed and swaying like reeds in the showers that now swept over the countryside.' Immediately after this, the foul paint-job preparation and transformation of the camp by the Nazis to make it look, for the benefit of Red Cross visitors, like a holiday resort, takes place, with the almost-inference that it was this moment of simile slippage, in a novel whose subject is the telling of truths, which made this fabrication possible.

'In the very essence of poetry there is something

indecent,' Czesław Miłosz says in his poem *Ars Poetica?*
(translated into English by himself and Lillian Vallee):

> a thing is brought forth which we didn't know we had
>     in us,
> so we blink our eyes, as if a tiger had sprung out
> and stood in the light, lashing its tail. . . .

> The purpose of poetry is to remind us
> how difficult it is to remain just one person,
> For our house is open, there are no keys in the doors,
> and invisible guests come in and out at will.

> What I'm saying here is not, I agree, poetry,
> as poems should be written rarely and reluctantly,
> under unbearable duress and only with the hope
> that good spirits, not evil ones, choose us for their
>     instrument.

In the aesthetic act something comes to life. That's a
good phrase for it, *comes to life*, suggesting both something separate, apart from life, extra, from elsewhere, and
something not alive in the act of being invested with life.
The phrase *brought to life* does this same double take.

This is Graham Greene, on reading War and Peace: 'When I finished it, I felt, What's the use of ever writing again—since this has been done. The book was like some great tree, always in movement, always renewing itself.' (It didn't stop him writing, though.) This is what Katherine Mansfield wrote in note form inside her copy of Aaron's Rod by DH Lawrence: 'There are certain things in this book I do not like. But they are not important, or really part of it. They are trivial, encrusted, they cling to it as snails to the underside of a leaf—no more,—and perhaps they leave a little silvery trail, a smear, that one shrinks from as from a kind of silliness. But apart from these things is the leaf, is the tree, firmly planted, deep thrusting, outspread, growing grandly, alive in every twig. All the time I read this book I felt it was feeding me.'

## 3: Putting the I's in Proliferation: Form and Multiplicity

This section was hardly formed at all. It was just handwritten notes. There was a passage from Katherine Mansfield about a whole hotel's-worth of selves all combining

to make just one single self, and a note from Virginia
Woolf about the vital importance of being more than one
gender: 'It is fatal to be a man or woman pure and simple;
one must be woman-manly or man-womanly . . . Some
marriage of opposites has to be consummated.' Then
there was a name, underlined. Kusama. Japanese? There
was a quote after her name: 'By continuously reproduc-
ing the forms of things that terrify me, I am able to
suppress the fear.'

Kusama, I worked out from your notes, was a Japanese painter from the twentieth century, still painting
now in the twenty-first; you had written down a story
about how when she was a young woman her mother, furi-
ous at her because she wouldn't give up her ambition to
be an artist, kicked her paint-palette across the room.
Color must have spilled everywhere, you wrote. Then you
had noted how what Kusama ended up doing was not just
making marks on a canvas but bleeding out over the edge
of that canvas into the rest of the room with the colors
and the marks she was making; she worked with net
shapes and polka dots, tiny dots and squiggles which
looked like minuscule fish or sperm, or cells or eggs or
eyes, or microbes or tiny planets, and she would cover a
huge canvas (and then go over the edge into the rest of

the space) in these forms, which a viewer would think looked mechanized, repetitive, and identical until, examined close-up, it'd become apparent that each and every one was different.

After this, you'd written the single word in capitals, CÉZANNE, and left the rest of the page blank. The next page, which was the last page of On Form, had a scrawl on it, difficult to read. Did that say Italic? Italian? Cumin? Italian Cumin says near end of his book Six Memos that letters of the alphabet, words, literatures, are combinations, 'pages of signs, packed as closely together as groins of [must be grains of] sand, representing the many-colored spectacle of the world on a surface that is always the same and always different, like dunes [slitted?] by the desert wind.' Oh, it was Calvino, it was Italo Calvino, because below that scrawl was a photocopy cut out and stapled on to the page, and it said his name underneath. 'Think what it would be to have a work conceived from outside the *self*, a work that would let us escape the limited perspective of the individual ego, not only to enter into selves like our own but to give speech to that which has no language, to the bird perching on the edge of the gutter, to the tree in spring and the tree in fall, to stone, to cement, to plastic . . .'

The staple was rusty, which made me wonder about the damp status of the study at home. I looked at the way your writing sat next to the print of the photocopied text. It made me think about what writing was, seeing them together like that. It was very difficult to read, your writing—I mean, it had always been difficult, but had clearly become even more difficult at this point in your life, the point at which you'd been making these notes; I could see how it must have been painful to write.

Look at its curves, though, its lovely jerky slopes. Look at your y's and your g's. Look at the way you ran *ing* at the end of *representing* into a penciled line with no discernible letters in it at all. No one had handwriting like it. It could only be your hand.

I got up off the bed, I went over to the laptop and opened it, it glowed straightaway into life. I typed in the word Kusama. I looked back at your sleeping form, the trick of the dark.

A photo of a young woman with a paintbrush, standing waist deep in a river or a lake, came up on to the screen. Was she really trying literally to paint a river? A smudge of redness wisped away from her, disappearing into the water.

Then it struck me that maybe I could fill it in for you,

the stuff you hadn't had the chance to say about Cézanne, in the space you'd left under the word CÉZANNE.

I tried to remember what you'd ever said about him or his work. I knew we'd seen some of his paintings, and that you loved them. We'd stood in front of one of his pictures in a quiet gallery in a grand building in London, a place full of the most beautiful paintings and almost nobody but us there looking at them, and you'd told me the story about how Cézanne would slash and burn his own canvases in a fury, or when his child poked holes in them would exclaim with delight, look! he's given it windows! he's opened up the chimney!; how one day he threw something he was working on, a study of apples, out of the window of the top floor of his house and it landed in the branches of a fruit tree below, and he left it for weeks, till the day he looked up, saw it again and called to his son to go and get the ladder because it had ripened enough for him to work on it a bit more.

The painting we were standing in front of when you told me this, a painting of a lake and some trees, was so full of the color green that it's almost all I remember about it, that greenness, though I remember you pointing out to me how everything in the picture was treated with the same importance or lack of importance, how every slab or flick of color mattered as much as every other, that that's how the painting made its shapes, and how it mattered, too, that we knew it *was* a painting, something made, how Cézanne had wanted people who saw it to see how it was formed out of paint, made of color, made of surface, before they even thought about trees or a lake. That way, you said, the artifice was what made the place in the picture—as well as the picture—truly alive. That way, we knew that it was telling us no lies, it was not deluding us, it was real.

In the space under CÉZANNE, I wrote, instead, with my own handwriting next to yours:

*I have been reading Charles Dickens's novel Oliver Twist, I am halfway through it, roughly. (Oliver has just been shot in the arm, which is something I had totally forgotten happens.) I was interested to read in it so often about the color green. It is practically the first thing the Artful Dodger calls Oliver when he meets him, green, and 'Greenland' is where the Dodger tells the boys back at Fagin's that Oliver's come from, and the first thieving act that Oliver sees happen and then gets blamed for happens on The Green when Charley and the Dodger rob a man in a green coat, Mr. Brownlow, which suggests there is a relationship about knowing and not knowing between Mr. Brownlow and Oliver.*

I put the hotel pencil down and went over to get Oliver Twist from the bedside cabinet. I flicked through it till I found the moment he and the Dodger meet.

'Hullo, my covey! What's the row?' said this strange young gentleman to Oliver.

'I am very hungry and tired,' replied Oliver, the tears standing in his eyes as he spoke. 'I have walked a long way. I have been walking these seven days.'

'Walking for sivin days!' said the young gentleman. 'Oh, I see. Beak's order, eh? But,' he added, noticing Oliver's look of surprise, 'I suppose you don't know what a beak is, my flash com-pan-i-on?'

Oliver mildly replied, that he had always heard a bird's mouth described by the term in question.

'My eyes, how green!' exclaimed the young gentleman. 'Why, a beak's a madgst'rate; and when you walk by a beak's order, it's not straightforerd, but always a going up, and nivir a coming down agin. Was you never on the mill?'

It's like literality meeting a metaphor, I thought. Or—
no—it's like a real apple meeting a Cézanne apple. It's as
if the Dodger speaks another language altogether; and
it's as if Oliver *has* to understand that a beak can be more
than one thing, and a mill, and all the words that come
in the paragraph after too, a stone jug, a magpie. Everything can be more than itself. Everything IS more than
itself. When he understands that words are more than
literal, then his own second name becomes the twist of
his own story, one that can eventually deliver the right
ending, the true identity to a lost and homeless boy. 'We
name our fondlings in alphabetical order. The last was
a S,—Swubble, I named him. This was a T,—Twist, I
named *him.*' Oliver Twist, far from being named ran-
domly, has actually been named according to the order of
the materials that make language, the basis of the writing
down of words.

My eyes! How green. I liked it that although I thought
I knew this story, reading it again had become a finding
of things I'd had no idea were in it. I liked how when
he meets 'the Artful,' the book really comes alive, almost *because* he begins to understand about colorful language, and I liked how Dickens called the Dodger all his
names, the Artful, the Dodger, the Artful Dodger, Jack

Dawkins, Mr. John Dawkins, like he was a work of shifting possibility. I liked how the Artful Dodger's cocked hat was always so unsafe on the top of his head but still stayed there anyway, never fell off, was all about balance. I liked how Fagin and the boys taught Oliver about theater—taught him their thievery by giving performances so funny that this boy, whose existence has been so pitiful, and who has done so much crying and trembling and swooning throughout the novel till then, sits laughing at their performances until the tears run out of his newly opened eyes.

I fell asleep at the hotel writing desk and when I woke up it was morning, the light was very bright out there in Brighton behind the window blind, and something fundamental in me must have altered overnight because I had pulled that blind up, had opened the window, had looked up at the sky, had washed my face, had had breakfast, had gone out into the air and had walked a length of the seafront before I even remembered that I had an old life, before it struck me again that I was alone.

# On edge

The art of losing isn't hard to master;
so many things seem filled with the intent
to be lost that their loss is no disaster.

Lose something every day. Accept the fluster
of lost door keys, the hour badly spent.
The art of losing isn't hard to master.

Then practice losing farther, losing faster:
places, and names, and where it was you meant
to travel. None of these will bring disaster.

I lost my mother's watch. And look! my last, or
next-to-last, of three loved houses went.
The art of losing isn't hard to master.

I lost two cities, lovely ones. And, vaster,
some realms I owned, two rivers, a continent.
I miss them, but it wasn't a disaster.

– Even losing you (the joking voice, a gesture
    I love) I shan't have lied. It's evident
    the art of losing's not too hard to master
though it may look like (*Write* it!) like disaster.

(ELIZABETH BISHOP, One Art)

One day in the middle of winter I was on my way home when I stopped in the street because I couldn't think why I was bothering to go home. I crossed the road because a bus was coming, heading in the opposite direction from home.

In the bus shelter there was a boy of about fifteen. He had no jacket on, even in this cold weather. His nose was running. His arms were pale with cold; I know because he was wearing a tee shirt. The tee shirt had these words written on it: I'm so broke I can't even pay attention.

The bus came. The boy with the word broke on his chest got on it. I sat down where he'd been; the plastic ridge they give you to sit on in bus shelters was still warm from him.

I looked down at the pavement, where the ash from the cigarette he'd been smoking was blowing about where his feet had been. I looked across at the line of skeletal municipal saplings over the road outside the insurance offices. Plane trees. City trees are great. They coat their own leaves with stuff that means that every time it rains any pollution that's gathered on them just slides off. Even those spindly young trees, they'd see themselves through the winter fine.

The thing about trees is that they know what to do. When a leaf loses its color, it's not because its time is up and it's dying, it's because the tree is taking back into itself the nutrients the leaf's been holding in reserve for it, out there on the twig, and why leaves change color in autumn is because the tree is preparing for winter, it's filling itself with its own stored health so it can withstand the season. Then, clever tree, it literally pushes the used leaf off with the growth that's coming behind it. But because that growth has to protect itself through winter too, the tree fills the little wound in its branch or twig where the leaf was with a protective corky stuff that seals it against cold and bacteria. Otherwise every leaf lost would be an open wound on a tree and a single tree would be covered in thousands of little wounds.

Clever trees. Know-it-all trees. I was tired of trees. I looked up at the sky. It was there, like it always was, like it always would be. It was regardless. It had no eyes for anything but itself. Cut me open with a knife the color of that January sky, take a sliver of sky as sharp as a cheese-wire and split me down the center from here at the top of my head, and what would be inside?

I went to the doctor and told him I needed help with mourning.

Would you say you're near the edge? he said. Because if you are, you can have six free sessions with a counselor.

The counselor wrote down the words *seeing, dead* and *partner.*

Yes, always turning up, and not just round the house, I said, elsewhere too, all over the place.

(In actuality, you'd been turning up less and less. Actually you'd not been back since I went to Brighton three months ago. But I wasn't going to tell her that.)

And how do you feel about that? she said. Well, I said, obviously I'm imagining it. It's obviously part of the mourning process, no? What exactly do you see? she asked. I told her about you stealing things from the house, and how the things were getting bigger, that you were now stealing quite large things, had even taken the hoover plus its nozzle attachments (though the truth was, since October all I'd missed were a couple of plastic tubs of homemade soup out of the freezer and it was possible that you hadn't taken these at all, that I'd merely eaten them myself and then forgotten I had when I next looked in the freezer). I told her about your habit of turning up whenever you liked, even if it was inconvenient for me (I didn't tell her how most of the times when you'd come back all you'd done was sit in the study staring at those old unfinished talks piled on the desk, saying nothing, nothing at all, to me).

That must be very frustrating for you, she said. Tell me more about it. Oh always barging in, I said, forever interrupting me telling me all about wherever it is that the dead people go, telling me made-up words too, I mean, how fantastic *is* the imagination? My dead lover doesn't just come back to life but speaks to me in a made-up language. Great-sounding words, I mean, they almost sound like they *should* be real: epomony, guide a ruckus, trav a brose, spoo yattacky, clot so scoofy, but that's what marriage is, isn't it? someone coming home and telling you their half-stories about their day, telling you things you don't really understand, same as they wouldn't understand if we were to tell them our stuff, I mean the number of times I came home and held forth about the complex relationship between roots of trees and the roots of the Amanita muscaria, the Lepiota cristata, the Boletus elegans, know what I mean?

The counselor had stopped and picked up the pen again; she was sitting forward holding it poised above a notepad.

I don't think they're nonsense words, she said.

No, they're toadstools, I said.

I mean the other words, she said. The words you said first. The words you said were a nonsense language. I don't think they are.

It's really nice of you, I said. I know, I like to think they mean something too, I like to imagine they mean all sorts of lovely things. But, you know, my partner worked a lot with words and I think it's like my imagination is really letting that go, allowing things *not* to mean after all.

Greek to me, the counselor said.

Ha ha, me too, definitely all Greek to me, I said.

No, I mean really Greek, the counselor said. And not ancient Greek. Modern Greek.

Oh, I said.

I don't mean to bring personal information into the

session room and it's especially unusual for me to do so in an initial session, the counselor said. But it just so happens that my husband's Greek.

Oh, I said. Right.

And that first word you said, she said. What was it again? I don't remember, I said. (I did remember, but I was now a bit annoyed.) The word that sounded like economy, she said. Epomony, I said. Yes, she said, that word, that sounds like a word he says a lot. Are you mixing it up with the word economy, I mean thinking it sounds Greek because of the present state of the economy? I said. No, the word he says is definitely epomony, she said, actually, it's a word he often sings. Sings? I said. In the shower, the counselor said. But I can't speak Greek, I said. I don't know any Greek words, or any Greek people. I've never even been to Greece. Tell me the words again, she said, and I'll make a note of them and check with him.

I told her the words I could remember and she wrote things down.

Now, she said. Where were we?

But why would *you* know that, about them maybe being Greek, and *I* wouldn't? I said.

It must be very frustrating for you, the counselor said.

I looked at this woman and I thought to myself, she

hasn't lost anything. She's never been left unsure about a single thing. She has a husband. He sings in the shower. I must have been looking at her with bare hostility because she shifted in her chair.

You appear to be very on edge, she said. I'm actually absolutely fine actually, I said. How would you feel about trying a short relaxation technique? she said. If I have to, I said. You don't have to do anything, she said. No, no, sure, okay, I said, I mean, relaxation's always good, isn't it, it's very, uh, relaxing.

She told me to sit back and close my eyes, then starting at the tips of my toes she talked me through all the parts of my body, telling me to ask them each to relax. Then she said, imagine it's a summer's day.

It's January, I said.

Imagine it's summer, she said, and imagine a warm place, somewhere where you feel completely safe. Maybe the place is in the countryside. Look all round you at the place, stand and turn and look 360 degrees round you. Then—can you see—down the path there, there's a gate.

Right, a gate, I said.

Now you go through the gate, and you follow the path, she said, and listen for all the sounds you hear, and how you can hear the sound of the sea in the distance. Walk towards the shore, looking and listening all round you as you go. Eventually there it is, a beach, and you're totally safe, it's very peaceful, it's a wonderful place. Now. What's the sea like?

I have no idea, I said. I'm still way back at that gate. At the gate? she said. Open it and walk through it. I can't, I said. Try, she said. I just can't, I said. Ah, the counselor said. Um. Nobody's ever stopped off at the gate when I've done this technique before.

Should I open my eyes? I said. No, no, keep them closed, she said. Okay, um—. Okay, I know. Wait a minute. We're going to try another technique, a specific self-empowerment technique. Right. Now. Turn from the gate and, em, right, you're walking along the road, okay?

Away from the gate? I said.

Yes, she said, away in the opposite direction, and you walk along until you come to a cinema.

Right, I said. Do I go in?

Yes, she said, you go in, and you go through to the auditorium and you see the rows of seats stretching away ahead of you, and—. Don't I have to get a ticket? I said. Yes, yes, the counselor said, you've got all that sorted—. What number is my seat? I said. Don't worry about that kind of thing, she said, just—. No, I'm not worried, I said, it's just that when I go to the cinema I like to sit at the end of the row so I can leave if I want and so I don't feel too crowded—. There's no one else in the whole cinema, she said, just you, so you can go anywhere you like, sit any—. But the film'll be rubbish if there's no one else in the cinema, I said. I probably wouldn't stay if I saw that there was no one else.

The counselor sighed.

Okay, I said. Okay, I'm in the auditorium. It's nice. Very modern.

Right, she said, and there's a curtain, and it's drawing up to reveal the screen and the lights are dimming, because something's about to begin. Okay with that? Yes, I said. The curtain and the lights, yes, I'm there, uh huh.

She talked on and on. She told me I was sitting in the dark and that there was a light playing on the screen, and to think about how what I saw on the screen was a certain situation, any situation of my choice that I felt out of control about.

Okay, I said. (As if seeing something on a screen would give me any power over anything.)

She told me to imagine I was there in it, the situation, whatever it was, and also sitting watching it. Then she told me to rewind the film I was watching, to watch it playing backwards then play it forwards again, but this time without any sound. Then to rewind it and start it again and see it, the same thing, but this time in black and white. Then to rewind and watch it in close-up, then rewind and watch it slowed down, then rewind and watch it on fast-forward.

I nodded, I pretended to do as she said. But instead of imagining her film going backwards and forwards, I found I was thinking about how much I was missing making love with you.

When we made particularly good love it was as if a new place in the world, or maybe a new place *out* of the world, a place apart, revealed itself, a landscape just rolling itself open, in my head—was it in my head? because it was all around me, a great unfolding green landscape, and it'd be as if I was traveling fast through it and over it in flight, skimming it like a flat-edged stone can skim a surface of water, touching it to leap away above it. I thought how somewhere at the core of this lovemaking I had sometimes known, understood for a moment, what goes on at the core of the earth down through all the roots, past the taproots, way down through the layers of cold to the layers of heat, right through to platelet level. I thought, too, how at exactly the same time as going this deep I could understand any huge bell hung high in a bell tower, hollow and full, stately and weighty, as high in the air as a bird, beginning the slow ceremonious swing of itself against itself that means any second the air is going to change its nature and become sound.

It was a place that could only be reached when you were brave enough to come into yourself so wholly that you left yourself behind.

It was a place I missed. I had no idea how to get back to it. I had no idea if I'd ever see it or be in it again.

And that's where the projector stops whirring, the counselor was saying, and the lights come up, and you stand up and you leave the cinema and come out into the daylight, and now you can open your eyes.

I opened my eyes.

There, the counselor said. Now. How was that? Did anything come of that?

I thought about the place I'd remembered. I thought how beautiful, and how beyond me.

It rang a bell with me somewhere, yes, I said.

I was sitting at home in the study, at the desk. I was two-thirds of the way through Oliver Twist. The bad, lost, poor, desperate, filthy, hopeless girl from the underworld, Nancy, had just met the good, perfect, rich, clean paragon of a girl from the overworld, Rose. Was there such a word as overworld? I picked up your dictionary. Under it were your unfinished talks. The one on the top of the pile was the one called On Edge.

No, there was no word *overworld* listed in the dictionary. But how could there be an underworld and no overworld? Was it just that Rose's world is so much more superior to Nancy's that there's no need even to label it? Then again, when Nancy comes to the door of the overworld—'like a corpse come to life again,' Sikes says of her as she gets ready to go there—and asks to 'see the lady' so she can tell her the truth about Oliver, a man asks her what her name is and she says, 'It's no use saying any.'

Maybe the languages of underworld and overworld can't really meet, I thought, opening the old paperback wider, cracking the spine on it, hearing the gum of the binding give. Maybe that's why you'd been giving me messages in a language I couldn't speak and I knew for sure you couldn't speak either.

On top of your unfinished talk about edge there was a folded photocopy. I unfolded it; it was a black and white picture of four young women, all of them very pretty, even beautiful, and all of them leaning on each other in a couple of deck chairs. Two of them were holding up dainty cups on dainty saucers and all four of them in the picture were completely asleep. The caption at the bottom said: Surrealists at Lambe Creek, Cornwall 1937. Clockwise from top left: Lee Miller, Ady Fidelin, Nusch Eluard, and Leonora Carrington.

One day, quite late on, you showed me this photograph; you must have been working on it at the time. You told me about how Lee Miller, the very beautiful woman at the top of the photograph, had started as a Surrealist photographer then in the Second World War had taken photographs all over Britain which still looked like they were Surrealism except now they were realism. Then, you said, she went into France and Germany at the end of the war with the Allies, she photographed the Liberation, she photographed the first ever use of napalm, and she was one of the first photographers into the concentration camps. You went and got a book off the shelf and came back with it. You showed me a pyramid made of shadow, a slit of light in a piece of netting, a woman with a disembodied hand on the back of her head, a typewriter crushed like a concertina. You turned the pages: a dead man in water, a train carriage with bare-chested, loose-armed corpses spilling out of its sliding door. You stopped at a picture of a blonde girl, authoritative, like a soldier or a nurse, leaning back on a couch. Look, you said. Eight years later Miller took this one. The girl is the daughter of the Leipzig Bürgermeister, she's just committed suicide.

The girl in this photo looked like she was asleep too, but the layer of dust on her lips and her face, on her perfect row of teeth, dust from the streetfighting and the explosions, meant that now she was just another surface in the room.

You told me how Miller's photographs had been lost, completely forgotten about in the final decades of her life, while her husband, who'd taken the photo of the four sleeping women holding the cups, Roland Penrose, carried on being the important figure he was in Surrealism and British art. Then one day, some time after her death, her son's wife went up into the loft and found thousands of negatives, and a set of astonishing and vivid written dispatches she'd sent from the front to Vogue, who'd published them, in the war's final push.

Then you'd pointed at the dark-haired woman sitting lowest in the picture. That's Leonora Carrington, you said, one of the most underrated of the British Surrealist artists and writers. Why we haven't had a huge retrospective of her work at the Tate I don't know. Best known, because she was Max Ernst's lover, as a Surrealist wild-child and muse. But her own work is unique, startling, completely original, a cutting-edge all on its own.

That night in bed you showed me some of Carrington's pictures. They were dark and bright, playful, like pictures from stories, but wilder, more savage, full of sociable-looking animals and wild-looking animals, beings who were part animal and part human, looking like they were all having a very interesting conversation, masked beings, people who were turning into birds or maybe it was birds turning into people. You got up and left the room, came back through with another couple of books. You opened one at a story called As They Rode Along the Edge. It was about a parsimonious saint who tries to fool a lot of clever creatures, led by a wild hairy girl called Virginia Fur, into letting the church have not just their souls but their bodies. Virginia Fur spends her time, followed by a large number of cats, whizzing about at great speed on a single wheel, in a balancing act on the borderline between divine and bestial where it soon becomes apparent that saintliness is pretty beastly and that animals have real spirit.

You flicked further into the book and read me this: 'However deeply we look into each other's eyes a transparent wall divides us from explosion where the looks cross outside our bodies. If by some sage power I could capture that explosion, that mysterious area outside where the wolf and I are one, perhaps then the first door would open and reveal the chamber beyond.'

It sounds like it could be good and it sounds like it could be bad, I said. It sounds ceremonious.

You told me Leonora Carrington was an expert in liminal space. What's liminal space? I'd asked you. Ha, you'd said. It's kind of in-between. A place we get transported to. Like when you look at a piece of art or listen to a piece of music and realize that for a while you've actually been somewhere else because you did? I'd said. Or liminal like limbo? Maybe, you'd said, getting excited, wait, I'll look it up, maybe limbo and liminal share a root, it sounds like they might.

I'd started singing the Doris Day song called Let the Little Girl Limbo, which we had on an album of lost songs of the early 1960s, it was a song her husband/manager had banned her from releasing and you and I had listened to it in bewilderment trying to work out why. Because limbo was too sexy? Because it rhymes with *go so low*, and he didn't want anyone to think Doris Day would? I said. You thought it was probably because it sounded too Afro-Caribbean, too close to an ethnic border for the marketing men to take a chance on in the early 60s.

Now, sitting at the desk, with you well beyond whatever liminal was and me stuck firmly in the overworld, I looked at that picture of the four sleeping women. I wondered who the other two women were and what had happened to them in their lives. In the picture it looked as if they'd all been having tea together and a spell, a sleeping enchantment, had been cast on them. The two women in the middle of the picture, the two not holding the cups, looked like they were actually getting a lot done in their sleep. They didn't look unhappy, no, they looked serious, as if sleep was a serious business, even a kind of work rather than something peaceful or absenting. In fact, it was as if sleep had made them even more there—or differently there.

In Oliver Twist there were a couple of times when Oliver was in a sleeping/waking state. In one, he's miles from his old life, safe in a lovely upper-class house with the Maylies, and suddenly, in his half-sleep, 'a kind of sleep that steals upon us sometimes, which . . . holds the body prisoner,' he knows for sure that Fagin and Monks are just beyond the window, just the other side of it. So he's still not safe, regardless of how safe it seems in the country with the Maylies. He's still not free. There was another description of that sleep state much earlier in the novel—a much more empowering-sounding one:

> a drowsy state, between sleeping and waking, when you dream more in five minutes with your eyes half open, and yourself half conscious of everything that is passing around you, than you would in five nights with your eyes fast closed, and your senses wrapt in perfect unconsciousness. At such times, a mortal knows just enough of what his mind is doing, to form some glimmering conception of its mighty powers, its bounding from earth and spurning time and space, when freed from the restraint of its corporeal associate.

That's on his first night in Fagin's underworld; in this in-between state he 'sees' Fagin open a box of stolen watches, rings, bracelets, brooches, one with 'some very minute inscription on it,' exactly like the kind of thing that would be the proof of Oliver's true and stolen identity. I wondered, thinking of it now, whether that empowering sleep-vision meant that Dickens had maybe planned at one point for Oliver's mother's stolen jewelry to be in Fagin's box. I knew he was very much writing the story as he went along.

Empowering. See what happens when you enter therapy land? Everything gets therapeutic. I thought about that counselor I'd seen earlier today. I imagined her waking up and coming downstairs and finding someone has broken into her house, some small boy has been pushed through a window and has opened the door to thieves who've stolen her—her what? It didn't matter what; I just wanted to be able to imagine for a moment, on the face of someone who'd seemed to know better than I could how to decipher what was happening in my life, a passing shadow of the world I felt so close to and which she, and her husband who sang in the shower, who could speak a language I couldn't, and all the other people in the world whose lives were still so whole and simple and unmysterious, lived so very far from.

I needed drugs. I needed alcohol. I put my head down on the dictionary that had no word for overworld in it and wished I could fall asleep. In my sleep, I would stand up from the desk and pull on a coat. It would be like the one

Harpo Marx wears in the old Marx Brothers films, or the one Dickens describes the Artful Dodger wearing; it would be far too big for me, capacious and patched, tramplike, and as I buttoned it I'd come across a hidden pocket full of handkerchiefs knotted together like a magician's trick. I'd open the coat and run my hand down its inside lining, full of hidden pockets and compartments. I'd put my hand into one and pull out—what? a hand, on the end of an arm—a limb. A passport into limbo. The hand at the end of the arm would speak through a mouth made of thumb and first finger. You need to take me with you, it would say, so you don't come to no arm.

I'd pick it up and slip it back into its pocket and the hand, holding my own hand, would pull me deeper, my arm following, then my shoulder up to my neck, then my head then my other shoulder and finally the whole of me dropping for miles inside the pocket of the coat, I'd fall upside down cushioned by thick fabric, like sliding down the thick black folds of the kind of cloth an early photographer would use to cover his camera before and after exposing the plate, and when I hit the ground it would be like I'd fallen through black sky.

## 1. Edging Our Bets: the Glass Ceiling and the Frozen Sea

Are words on the page more than surface? Is the act of reading something a surface act? Do words on the page hold us on a surface, above depths and shallows like a layer of ice? (A book should be the axe to break the frozen sea inside us, Kafka says.) And what about reading on-screen—the latest, most modern way of communicating, working, writing a letter, writing a book, reading a book, telling a story?

What is a screen? A thing that divides. A thing people undress behind. A thing every computer has, in fact a thing computing has distilled itself increasingly into. A thing we all carry around with us in our pockets, a thing fundamental to western-world human information-gathering and a feature now fundamental—unimaginable this, only ten years ago—to a telephone. A thing that has an appearance of transparency and that divides us from bankers, ticket sellers, post office workers, people with money. A thing people project onto.

Does an image on a screen form the same kind of surface as words on a page? Filmmakers have been trying to conquer the way screens divide audiences from what they see on them since The Big Swallow in 1901, by James Williamson, where a man annoyed by a photographer taking his picture comes up so close to the camera that there's nothing but his mouth, which then swallows both camera and cameraman.

Straight after the opening credits of Chaplin's 1928 film The Circus, we see a hoop of paper with a star on it then a circus performer breaking through it. From the first appearance of his Tramp figure, in a 1914 short called Kid Auto Races at Venice, where he acts like what he looks like, a real member of the public who's trying to get into a film some newsreel men are making, Chaplin was keen to slice through any divisive filter between the audience and the form; and in The Circus especially (he's at the height of international fame when he makes it, probably still the most famous film symbol in the world) he wants to rip through any notions of stardom that might come between an audience and the everyman qual-ity of his Tramp figure.

Powell and Pressburger start each of their Archers films with a perfect screen circle too, with an archery target printed on it, already bristling with arrows, and into which an arrow flies in a virtuoso bull's-eye shot—

suggesting something is about to pass between watcher and screen that will hit home, hit the target. And Alfred Hitchcock knew very early that cinema screen and dream are related; he understood that the screen has to be permeable, pass-throughable, like Alice with the looking glass—that this permeable nature is what makes the screen a feasible mirror. In one of his British silent films, The Lodger (1927), a mysterious stranger moves into the house of a family whose members, like everybody in the city, are in a panic about a series of local murders. The lodger is strange, jumpy, weirdly energetic; he's not like anyone else. At one point the family stares up at a ceiling with a chandelier in it, and the ceiling turns to glass, you can see right through it, you can see the soles of the feet of the lodger, pacing up and down above them, because Hitchcock wants us to know what the family is hearing, the nervous pacing of the man on the floor above.

'I did it,' Hitchcock said afterwards, 'by having a floor made of one-inch-thick glass.' But it wasn't just a brainwave for showing sound visually in a silent film. Hitchcock, a brilliant early interpreter of film form, knew that to hook a film audience with real suspense you have to let them in on parts of the plot or understandings of narrative atmosphere that the people in the story can't have or understand. 'The whodunnit contains no emotion. The audience are wondering, they're not emoting, they're not apprehensive for anyone . . . When the film is finished and the revelation comes, well, you get two or three minutes of saying, 'ah, I told you so,' or 'I thought so,' or 'fancy that.' I prefer to do the suspense film by giving all the information to the audience at the beginning of the picture." Rarely among Hitchcock films, The Lodger doesn't do this, works on withheld knowledge— it's a film that Hitchcock didn't have full directorial choice over, because of the bankability of its star, Ivor Novello. But in his films that do, Hitchcock creates a psychological gray area where the division isn't between us and the story on the screen, it's between those who know and those who don't. In this way, knowledge becomes more than plot; it becomes a key to understanding action and morality.

In the first chapter of Henry James's The Golden Bowl (1904) the Prince, out for a walk in London, is a modern man from an ancient culture, an Italian about to marry a rich American, and is wandering Bond Street, window-shopping, looking through the 'plate glass all about him' at all the spoils of empire that money can buy, 'tumbled together' like 'loot.' Meanwhile the ladies pass him 'in faces shaded,' hidden by hats 'or more delicately tinted still under the tense silk of parasols.' He has his new-world marriage and his prospective father-in-law's millions to think about so he tells himself he doesn't need passion or love, that romance is a memory he can simply 'screen out—much as, just in front of him while he walked, the iron shutter of a shop, closing early to the stale summer day, rattled down at the turn of some crank.'

Poor Prince, foppishly wandering the city paying no attention to the clues in his own narrative; the heft of the novel is about to turn against him like a storm that thickens below the surface of a lake on which he thinks himself safe in his chic little boat. More—the churning storm at the heart of this novel will come in the form of a story about passion, about unmentionable love, and will be one that Henry James himself never once fully unveils, never allows to surface fully. The Golden Bowl is about worth, about money, about seeing the flaw in what looks perfect, yes. But as its first chapter insists, with its repeating imagery of veils and mists and screens and shutters and the shrouding these do, The Golden Bowl will be a narrative about a more deathly flaw, a state of blindness. James uses this resonant imagery to alert readers to something from which we're being withheld, to suggest to us to read beneath the surface a story whose absence is so pressing that we feel it through the narrative, bone beneath skin.

A hundred years after The Golden Bowl Javier Marías, in Volume 1 of his trilogy about surveillance and history, Your Face Tomorrow (translated by Margaret Jull Costa), has a visionary take on what living with screens is doing to human beings:

That is doubtless why television is such a success, because you can see and watch people as you never can in real life unless you hide … the screen gives you the opportunity to spy at your leisure and to see more and therefore know more, because you're not worrying about making eye contact or exposed in turn to being judged. … And inevitably you pass judgement, you immediately utter some kind of verdict (or you don't utter it, but say it to yourself), it only takes a matter of seconds and there's nothing you can do about it, even if it's only rudimentary and takes the least elaborate of forms, which is liking or disliking… And you surprise yourself by saying, almost involuntarily, sitting alone before the screen: 'I really like him,' 'I can't stand the guy,' 'I could eat her up,' 'He's such a pain,' 'I'd do anything he asked,' 'She deserves a good slap around the face,' 'Bighead,' 'He's lying,' 'She's just pretending to feel pity,' 'He's going to find life really tough,' 'What a wanker,' 'She's an angel,' 'He's so conceited, so proud,' 'They're such phonies, those two,' 'Poor thing, poor thing,' 'I'd shoot him this minute, without batting an eyelid,' 'I feel so sorry for her,' 'He drives me bloody mad,' 'She's pretending,' 'How can he be so naïve,' 'What a cheek,' 'She's such an intelligent woman,' 'He disgusts me,' 'He really tickles me.' The register is infinite, there's room for everything. And that instant verdict is spot-on, or so it feels when it comes (less so a second later). It carries a weight of conviction without having been subjected to a single argument. With not a single reason to sustain it.

In these one-liners, Marías isn't just parodying our screen culture. He is also parodying the movement of his own complex trilogy. As it develops it plays out in full what it means to be naïve, intelligent, a phony, lying, attractive, a wanker—and what it means not just to want to shoot someone without batting an eyelid, but for someone to stand—with no protection, nothing in between—

opposite another human being who means to do harm. On the one hand Your Face Tomorrow is about war, about the Spanish Civil War and its legacy, about the legacies of the twentieth century, and on the other it's about how we're seen, how we see. Its title plays on what it might be like to see—or not to see, because it's already too late— in tomorrow's newspaper, a picture of your own face, the latest victim of history, dead on the page.

It was photographs of the Spanish Civil War that galvanized Woolf, in her most political text, the antiwar polemic Three Guineas (1938), into becoming one of the first commentators on the ways in which a photograph will involve us and simultaneously distance us:

> Here then on the table before us are photographs. . . . They are not pleasant photographs to look upon. They are photographs of dead bodies for the most part. This morning's collection contains the photograph of what might be a man's body, or a woman's; it is so mutilated that it might, on the other hand, be the body of a pig.

The viewer's reaction is a kind of vacillation. It involves judgement that marks a certain level of distance ('not pleasant photographs') and, in the act of the inquiring glance and in the meld of understanding and deciphering, a reduction of human being to pig. In her writing about cinema a decade earlier, Woolf had already commented on how the exchange between eye and brain when watching cinema forms a separating surface between us and participation. She argued that what we see has become 'real with a different reality from that which we perceive in daily life[.] We behold [what we see in moving pictures] as they are when we are not there. We see life as it is when we have no part in it.'


## 2: Going Near the Edge: Depths, Borders, Bridges

Woolf was a great believer in art's capacity both to change things for us and to make visible crucial changes to us. 'On or about December 1910 human character changed,' she famously says in her 1924 essay Character in Fiction, in which she is challenging the novelist Arnold Bennett to a kind of realism duel and using Roger Fry's curation of the exhibition at London's Grafton Galleries, Manet and the Post-Impressionists, as fruitful evidence for the changes in the ways things were seen, in the ways of seeing. On or around July 1936, the year Woolf began writing Three Guineas, human character in London was getting its head round the First International Surrealist Exhibition, at the New Burlington Galleries, and Salvador Dalí, a figurehead for the edgiest of European art, was preparing his own head for a visit to new and dangerous depths:

A programme of lectures was organised, including Breton, Eluard and Dalí. Dalí decided to give his lecture in a diving suit and Edward James, with whom he was staying, took him to Siebe and Gorman, the renowned makers of hard-hat diving suits. The technician took Dalí very seriously, and inquired: 'Certainly sir, and for what depths do you require this suit?' To which Dalí replied: 'The depths of the subconscious!' He arrived at the gallery like a bug-eyed monster from the deep with a jewelled dagger in his belt and two borzois on a leash. Edward James, the collector of Surrealist art, positioned himself close by the helmet to translate Dalí's muffled words from Catalan to English, but could hear so little that the speech became more than usually incoherent. What did become quickly recognisable were Dalí's shouts for help as he began to suffocate inside the helmet. The helmet, secured against the extreme pressures of the subconscious, could not be released . . . The spanner was useless, but Edward James had been posing around with a billiard cue and that fitted neatly into the big brass loop on the nut which fastened the round window at the front of the helmet. Undoing it bought enough time to work out how to unscrew the helmet and save Dalí from becoming a more extreme event than even he had planned.

Edges involve extremes. Edges are borders. Edges are very much about identity, about who you are. Crossing a border is not a simple thing. Geopolitically, getting anywhere round the world in which we live now requires a constant producing of proof of identity. Who are you? You can't cross till we're sure. When we know, then we'll decide whether you can or not.

Edge is the difference between one thing and another. It's the brink. It suggests keenness and it suggests sharpness. It can wound. It can cut. It's the blade—but it's the blunt part of the knife too.

It's the place where two sides of a solid thing come together. It means bitterness and it means irritability, edginess, and it means having the edge, having the advantage. It's something we can go right over. It's something we have on someone or something when we're doing better than him or her or it. It's something we can set teeth on. And if we take the edge off something, we're making something more pleasant—but we're also diminishing it.

There's always an edge, in any dialogue, in any exchange. There's even an edge in monologue, between the speaker and the silent listener. In fact there's an edge in every meeting, between every thing about to come together with something beyond it.

Edges are magic, too; there's a kind of forbidden magic on the borders of things, always a ceremony of crossing over, even if we ignore it or are unaware of it. In medieval times weddings didn't take place inside churches but at their doors—thresholds as markers of the edge of things and places are loaded, framed spaces through which we pass from one state to another. In the eighteenth century people found that standing on the edge of a cliff or a sheer drop was a very good way to view what became known as the sublime; a hundred years later Gerard Manley Hopkins wrote about the edge as a force of psychological sublimity, how 'the mind, mind has mountains; cliffs of fall / Frightful, sheer, no-man-

fathomed. Hold them cheap / May who ne'er hung there';
for the notion of edge is double-edged, involves notions of
survival and a natural proximity to words like *over the.*

'It is at the edge of the / petal that love waits,' William Carlos Williams writes in The Rose Is Obsolete, a
poem that begins by declaring overness, something finished, a poetic and a natural obsolescence, but immediately moves on to become a poem about the renewal
of both natural power and aesthetic symbolism when it
comes to an old bloom, an old poetic cliché, the flower of
love, the rose:

Crisp, worked to defeat
laboredness—fragile
plucked, moist, half-raised
cold, precise, touching

What

The place between the petal's
edge and the

From the petal's edge a line starts
that being of steel

infinitely fine, infinitely

rigid penetrates

the Milky Way

In his poem's performance of spontaneous internal dis-
cursiveness, Williams opens to renewal everything that
appears complete or perfected. Even things which seem
separate and finished are infinitely connected and will
infinitely connect, the poem suggests, and this connec-
tion happens as soon as you let it, as soon as you engage—
as soon as you even attempt to engage.

To William Carlos Williams, thought is a connective
bridge. It's by appearing on London Bridge that Nancy, in
Dickens's Oliver Twist, can signal to the upper-class characters that she's still alive. It's 'on the Bridge of Peace' that
W. G. Sebald's narrator, in his poem-sequence After Nature, finally pieces together the fragments of the past. But
when he does it brings him close to madness, for the bridge
is the drawn line between unresolved or unreconciled
existences—it suspends you between edges, in midair.

In the opening lines of José Saramago's novel The
Stone Raft, 'when Joana Carda scratched the ground with
the elm branch' all the dogs for miles around began to
bark, in line 'with the fable that in mythological times of

ancient Greece, here, in the district of Cerbère in the Eastern Pyrenees,' the three-headed mythical dog after whom the place has been named would start a similar barking, with all three of his heads presumably, whenever his master, Charon, ferryman of the dead across the River Styx, summoned him. The line Joana Carda draws, we find out later, gesturally signifies the end of a relationship between herself and a lover. But what happens when she draws this line (and simultaneously when another couple of characters do another couple of random things, one skims a stone, one simply stands up from sitting in a chair) is that a crack appears in the fabric of Europe, and as this crack grows, Europe literally starts to break up. 'Who can tell what tomorrow may bring, the Pyrenees appeared to be solid for all eternity, and look what happened.' Administrators from Spain and France rush to fill the crack with concrete and as soon as they start to celebrate their mending job the concrete disappears down an even wider hole and the crack gets bigger, becomes an edge, the Iberian Peninsula pulls against the thick ropes that the powers-that-be have strung across the abyss, the ropes break

like ordinary string, some that were stronger uprooted the trees and posts to which they were tied. Then

there was a pause, a great gust of air could be felt
rushing through the air, like the first deep breathing
of someone awakening, and the mass of stone and
earth, covered with cities, villages, rivers, woodlands,
factories, wild scrub, cultivated fields, with all their
inhabitants and livestock, began to move, a ship drawing away from harbor and heading out to an unknown
sea once more

—something beyond us and alive to change asserts itself
and a piece of what used to be mainland Europe simply
floats off by itself, and it must matter that Saramago's
first reference, first connecting bridge, first linking motif
on his first page of this novel of breakage, is to magic, to
myth, and to the divide between the living world and the
world of the dead.

Is it a coincidence that Michael Powell's first major
feature, Edge of the World (1937), about the very edge of
the British Isles, what the Romans called Ultima Thule,
happens to have the ladies of the Glasgow Orpheus Choir
singing over its opening credits? Here's another Glasgow
Orphean moment, from Edwin Morgan. Orpheus is full
of joy; his dead love, Eurydice, is behind him, being led
back to the surface of the world from the underworld by

the messenger god Hermes (or Mercury), coming back to
the surface of life because Orpheus's music has moved
Hades and Persephone into letting her go—on the condition that, on their way between the worlds, Orpheus does
not once look behind to see her:

> five hundred million hummingbirds sat in the Kelvin Hall / three
> hundred thousand girls took double basses
> in a crocodile to Inverkip / six thousand children drew Rothesay
> through twelve thousand kites / two hundred
> plumbers with morning cellos galvanized the bedmakers of Fairlie
> / forty babies
> threw their teething-rings at a helicopter / trickety-track / till
> Orpheus looked back
> and there was nothing but the lonely hills and sky unless the
> chilling
> wind was something / and the space
> of pure white pain where his wife had held his hand from hell / he
> left the place
> and came to a broken shack at midday / with carts and horses /
> strong
> dark ragged boys
> played in the smoke / the gypsies gave him soup and bread / for
> the

divine brooch / who cares

what is divine, he said /


and that's Orpheus displaced after this particular crossing of the wrong line, out on the edge of things with the gypsies, who never belong. Daring the divine line is always chancy, like it is in Rilke's Orpheus. Eurydice. Hermes., a poem whose title is already full of division and finality via the full stop which Rilke places after each name. Rilke suggests there's simply no point in trying to bring Eurydice back to the surface (here in Stephen Mitchell's translation):

> She had come into a new virginity
> and was untouchable; her sex had closed
> like a young flower at nightfall, and her hands
> had grown so unused to marriage that the god's
> infinitely gentle touch of guidance
> hurt her, like an undesired kiss.
>
> She was no longer that woman with blue eyes
> who once had echoed through the poet's
>     songs,

no longer the wide couch's scent and island,
and that man's property no longer.

She was already loosened like long hair,
poured out like fallen rain,
shared like a limitless supply.

She was already root.

Eurydice is over the edge; she has changed worlds. Sylvia Plath, in her poem Edge, one clearly heavily influenced by Rilke's Eurydice, is interested not just in ends and endings but in a continuing aesthetic tradition of finishings and of tragic completion.

The woman is perfected.
Her dead

Body wears the smile of accomplishment,
The illusion of a Greek necessity

Flows in the scrolls of her toga,
Her bare

Feet seem to be saying:
We have come so far, it is over.

Each dead child coiled, a white serpent,
One at each little

Pitcher of milk, now empty.
She has folded

Them back into her body as petals
Of a rose close when the garden

Stiffens and odors bleed
From the sweet, deep throats of the night flower.

The moon has nothing to be sad about,
Staring from her hood of bone.

She is used to this sort of thing.
Her blacks crackle and drag.

The starkness of the line after the word 'perfected'—two
words, 'Her dead' (followed four lines later by the match-
ingly stripped-back 'Her bare')—has brutal simplicity,

and when this is met by the rich complexity of satisfaction in its next line, the smile, then the accomplishment, a sense of control that's close to obscene, is suggested. But the poem, a refutal of fertility, is at the same time a gesture of Cleopatran panache; a refutal of the moons and roses of all poetry is at the same time a reclaiming of them, a remaking of them into indifference there on the edge between life and death, where the only continuity, suggested in the repeating assonance of the last line, is a diffident mourning.

There's no arguing with this Edge. It's practically set in stone. But in Alasdair Gray's novel 1982, Janine, a lonely man attempting suicide in a bed-and-breakfast room is physically ejected from his own death-attempt by an unexpected voice, one that has the edge on him. As the pills and the alcohol take their worst effect, the page breaks into columns then diamond-shaped text in a mix of typeface bolds and italics. Several voices speak at once. In the left-hand margin, the voice that speaks from the edge of the page argues back in a small squeezed typeface:

listen I came because you called and now your hot and cold floods of speech hardly allow me a word in

edgeways . . . listen I am not what you were told not an
owner true makers never own what they make I have
no authority that tool of high rabbles who live well by
serving the real makers badly I am not mysterious am
no king judge director inspector supervisor landlord
general manager or any kind of master no expert computer planner lawyer accountant clergyman policeman teacher doctor father who is cruel to be kind I do
not rule thunder threaten you will not leave you . . .
listen I am light air daily bread common human
warmth ordinary ground that drinks every stain takes
back all who fall renews all who have not poisoned
their seed my one power is letting nothing rest which
is not well balanced my only intelligence is what you
lend when you forget yourself

In Gray's work, physically, thematically, and politically,
the margins seethe with life, alive with an authority that
takes its power from refusing mainstream authority. His
first novel, Lanark (1981), was a juxtapositioning fusion
of futuristic fantasy and realism which changed the
chemical of both genres in the combination; in its Epi-
logue Gray filled the margins next to the main body of
the text with what he called his Index of Plagiarisms. He

included as a plagiarized source for chapter 47 (a chapter which doesn't exist) a complete short story in the margin of page 491, written by that other twentieth-century Scottish revivifier of fictional forms, James Kelman, and called Acid:

In this factory in the north of England acid was essential. It was contained in large vats.

Gangways were laid above them. Before these gangways were made completely safe a young man fell into a vat feet first. His screams of agony were heard all over the department. Except for one old fellow the large body of men was so horrified that for a time not one of them could move. In an instant this old fellow who was also the young man's father had clambered up and along the gangway carrying a big pole. Sorry Hughie, he said. And then ducked the young man below the surface. Obviously the old fellow had had to do this because only the head and shoulders . . . in fact, that which had been seen above the acid was all that remained of the young man.

Part joke, part apocrypha, part throwaway moment, part story which will gnaw at your bones, this discrete marginal moment is a demonstration of the edginess of edge, and of the power of editing, because the margins burn with the energy of the edit, being so pushed for space. 'I feel as fastidious as though I wrote with acid,' Katherine Mansfield—a New Zealander in exile in Europe, always a foreigner, always on the aesthetic edge of the group she called the Blooms berries, from her school days onwards always the outsider, 'the little colonial,' and still a marginal figure when it comes to how little she's considered in terms of canonical modernism, and in terms of how little critical attention the short story merits as a form—wrote this phrase in her notebook, while she worked at the stories whose sharpness of shape and whose bite would change the form of the short story, cross all the lines and draw their own defining line in the development of the form.

Literary vagrancy is what Mansfield saw in Robert Louis Stevenson, for whom traveling hopefully was better than arriving; the writer Elizabeth Hardwick's take on traveling, on the other hand, was this: 'when you travel your first discovery is that you do not exist.' 'One of the great Modernist writers of displacement,' the critic Lorna Sage called Mansfield, noting how in an average year she'd habitually change residence or city several times;

Sage even suggests that for Mansfield the short story form was the one place she 'felt at home . . . being so little at home anywhere else.'

## 3. Edge of the Woods: Putting the Us into Wandering Aengus

Here your talk broke down, like On Form broke down before it, into notes. I liked this broken place in you, but I'd loved reading you so fluently holding forth about screen. It was me who liked cinema, not you. We'd had a lot of arguments about it. And the thing about the Powell Pressburger target was something I'd actually once said to you. In fact, I'd said a lot of those things to you, about Chaplin and Hitchcock, and it was me who'd made you sit down with me and watch them both. I couldn't believe that what I'd said had got into your writing. It was thrilling. It felt fine. And I'd sat up straight in my seat when I got to the bit about Nancy on the bridge. It was like we were reading the same book, like you were just ahead of me in the reading.

What was left of On Edge was a poem you'd typed out and printed up: One Art, by Elizabeth Bishop. You'd written in pencil in the margin next to it, quite legibly for you, *the villanelle form holds all the lost things safe and simultaneously releases them, lets them be lost. NB how the level of loss builds to become a joke—until we get to the crux, the point, the prospect (way beyond, much worse than losing rivers and continents) of 'losing you.'*

I read the poem. It made me laugh. I liked how the poet dared herself, and how she was lying, making things rhyme. You'd clearly planned to compare a poem by Yeats about a man called Wandering Aengus who goes fishing, catches a beautiful girl on his line, then, when she disappears, vows to keep walking till he can find her and take her hand, with a poem by Stevie Smith called Fairy Story, about someone who goes into the woods, gets lost, meets a 'creature' who tells the speaker to sing a song, that singing a song will make the time pass, and that holding hands with him will make the speaker not be scared anymore. 'I sang a song, he let me go / But now I am home again there is nobody I know.' After this you'd written: *both poets left unhomed by their encounters with others; both encounters involving songs and hands.*

You'd written about a man in a Greek myth, I couldn't make out his name, who plays music so beautifully that the god Apollo challenges him to a music competition. If I win, Apollo says, then I get to skin you alive. The man agrees. *Of course the god wins*, you wrote, *because gods always win, but the music played by the man who is bound to lose his skin moves to tears, moves more than any god's perfect playing ever will, every living thing round him.* Under this Greek myth you'd written: *books and skins: books have spines because animals have spines—NB piece of leather forming fold of spine of book originally matched fold over spine of animal leather was cut from.*

I got up. I walked round the room, saw all the books there on all the shelves. I came through to the front room and I picked up the photo on the mantelpiece, the one of us in the garden, you pretending to fan me with the rhubarb leaf, huge and green, holding it by its stalk, bright red. The stalk is withered dry, my love. The photo meant you were dead.

But the photo kind of meant I was dead too.

God. If I had a chance to fetch you from the underworld, to go down and persuade them and fetch you home, I'd never look back.

But maybe you wouldn't want to come back. Maybe, like the woman in the poem, you were already root.

Maybe that was why not even my imagination could bring you back anymore.

Imagine that hand on the end of that arm. Imagine it talking. If it was your hand, it'd be being high-handed, it'd probably be talking of Michelangelo, saying something really intelligent like *do you remember the Michelangelo drawing I took you to see when it was on show, the one where the man is waking up from a dream? The beautiful man sitting on a box of masks, leaning on the large ball, the shape of which is a bit like buttocks or a peach—remember how he's wakened by the boy with wings hovering upside down above him and holding the slim trumpet so close to his forehead that you can almost feel the hairs prickle in the space in between? It's as if the man is being reborn, remember? But is he waking from a dream or is he waking into a dream?*

Ah, I'd let a hand like yours take me anywhere, even down a path strewn with bones like the floor of the cave I'd seen in the film by Werner Herzog, the Chauvet cave in France where they discovered all those tens-of-thousands-of-years-old animal pictures on the walls, the beautiful four heads of the horses, the creatures with long sweeps of horn. Above the bones the earliest ever art. Even on a path strewn with bones like that I'd be okay in your good hand.

It'd be as if we were walking through the inside of a skull, the rock in the cave all folded formations like glittering linen. Then we'd cross a river, I suppose, in a boat with a three-headed dog. I could use the hand and the arm as an oar. Then we'd get to a room littered with all the things you've taken from our house, all manner of things which we had in our life, all the old clothes and shoes, the old toothbrushes, all the squeezed-out old halves of orange, they'll all be there, like a junk shop of our lives, a bit like eBay, or the internet.

Then we'd pass through that, me on your arm, and into a dark room, three dark walls, one lit bright wall—the light would be coming from behind the wall, and I'd go to the wall and I'd cut through the wall with, I don't know, there's bound to be something back in the junk room I could use, an old penknife, something with an edge. I'd get through it anyhow. It's only a screen. There, beyond it, in a pure white space, you'd be standing like a figure in a holy picture. You wouldn't be broken any longer, or torn, or rotten, you'd be whole, beautiful, light would be coming off your head like off the heads of

Renaissance saints in paintings, great lines of gold, you'd be haloed in a kind of golden light like in the song by Beyoncé where she sings how she can see the person's halo and that person is her saving grace.

That's how cheap I am. That's how far I am from Michelangelo's Dream. That's what the mouth in the hand on the end of *my* too real arm would be doing, singing some trivial junk like Doris Day's Let the Little Girl Limbo, or something by Beyoncé. *Everywhere I'm looking now. I'm surrounded by your embrace. Standing in the light of your halo.*

Is that what liminal is? the light that came off you when I first saw you, that day when you walked past me? Because you were lit, you were lit by something, and it wasn't the usual kind of light, and you were so beautiful I almost had to leave that room, I swear your beauty was changing the surface of my skin.

Halo halo halo, what's goin' on 'ere then? I woke up and it was all a dream. No. More like: I never went to sleep and it was all still real.

So much for my Harpo Marx coat. Imagine Harpo Marx as the guide to the real twentieth-century underworld. Like Harpo Marx crossing a Brueghel painting. And so much for my Artful Dodger pockets. If I remem-

bered rightly, what was about to happen to him any minute in the story was that he'd mean less than a snuffbox
and they'd send him off to sea. Transported, that's the
word for it.

I picked up my copy of Oliver Twist to flick forward
and see—and the book fell apart in my hands. So I spent
some time trying to stick its pages and spine back into
readable form with cellotape. It wasn't till I was about to
get into bed and was plugging my phone in to recharge
that I saw I'd missed a message.

It was the counselor. Hello, she said, please accept
my apologies for calling you, again this is rather unprec-
edented, but I just wanted to let you know as soon as I
could that your language, the language we spoke about,
*is* a real one, and it does seem to be Greek. Epomony is
Greek for patience, as in having patience. Guide a ruckus
seems to mean little donkey. Spoo yattacky means small
sparrow. Trav a brose is a phrase that means move on, go
on, proceed, go to the front of things. There's one word
my husband says is untranslatable, what it really means
is a ball of rags or cloths tied together to make a football,
but by someone too poor or hopeless to be able to buy a
real ball, so in human terms it means an outsider, a fool,
a person on the edge of things, someone a bit too simple

who won't fit in, or an old-fashioned word like mooncalf. Clot so scoofy. And just one more thing. He says they're all songs, your words, and that they're all associated with one particular Greek actress.

Then she said a name I couldn't make out. Then she said goodbye, and the answerphone voice told me to press a number on my phone if I wanted to save the call for seven days.

I listened to the message again. A donkey? a sparrow? a mooncalf?

I got in on my side and put my head back onto the pillow. I stretched an arm and a leg over to your side of the bed. Then I moved my whole self to the middle of the mattress, actually the best place in the bed for a good night's sleep.

I closed my eyes.

Patience.

# On offer
# and on
# reflection

In my craft or sullen art

Exercised in the still night

When only the moon rages

And the lovers lie abed

With all their griefs in their arms,

I labor by singing light

Not for ambition or bread

Or the strut and trade of charms

On the ivory stages

But for the common wages

Of their most secret heart.


Not for the proud man apart

From the raging moon I write

On these spindrift pages

Nor for the towering dead

With their nightingales and psalms

But for the lovers, their arms

Round the griefs of the ages,

Who pay no praise or wages

Nor heed my craft or art.


(DYLAN THOMAS, In My Craft or Sullen Art)

There's always a first day in late winter—usually near the end of January though it depends how hard the winter's been—when the bare trunks of the trees shine green and the buds on the ends of the branches glow slightly brighter than the rest of the tree. It's the day the sapwood starts up working again, the xylem sap filling the trees' arteries, well, what trees have instead of arteries, with the fluids and minerals stored all winter in the roots.

Sapwood is the lighter, outer wood of a trunk, bound round the darker inner heartwood—which is formed of dead used-up sapwood. It's how trees grow.

Then there's always a first day in February when the daylight has so banked itself up against the dark that you can't not notice.

Then it's spring, March about to be April, the gardens throwing off a swath of winter-spring flowers, and then it's the first Monday after the clocks go forward, and it's light at seven o'clock. Who am I talking to? Who am I telling this to, the story that this year on that first light evening I was sitting in the front room watching a dvd of Oliver!, and when Mark Lester, who's been sold by Harry Secombe to Leonard Rossiter the undertaker, gets locked in a roomful of coffins, when he sits among the coffins singing the song about where is love, does it fall from skies above, is it underneath the willow tree that I've been dreaming of, when he goes to the barred window high in the wall of the cellar, sings his song leaning against it and then suddenly, unexpectedly, it gives—at that moment, this year, I realized that it was past seven o'clock and it was light outside again?

Off he goes to Covent Garden, to find all its fruits, all its flowers amazing to the eye after the workhouse and the undertaker's, but above all to coincide with Jack Wild, the Dodger, who works out it'll probably be to his advantage to befriend this runaway, so he steals a bread roll from a passing baker's tray, breaks a bit off for himself and throws the bulk of it to the hungry boy. Then the Dodger offers him accommodation, tells him to consider himself at home, one of the family, and leads him in such a merry dance that at the end of it the whole of London is up on its feet in an open festival of color and choreography.

This song and dance was, I knew when I was a child and saw this film, what happiness looked like, what happiness would be. Even now whenever I saw it again, moments of it still happened fresh to the eye, as if for the first time, though I'd seen the same thing so many times over. Like when the Dodger welcomes Oliver into the song, encourages him by singing the first half of a line and waiting to hear the new boy sing back the other half, which he does, like a question—like an answer met with a question: I knew this scene by heart but I'd never quite noticed that before.

You could so write about Oliver! I'd said to you when you were writing the last couple of those talks—well, when you were trying to, but were, you said, stuck, blocked. It wasn't surprising you were finding it hard, you weren't very well, and I'd come through to tell you to go easy on yourself. But saying that would have been like saying—well, I stood in the doorway and instead I said: you could so write about Oliver! in On Offer. He's on offer, in the film. There's a whole song about it. Boy for

Sale. The price keeps coming down because nobody'll take him, and in the end when the undertaker gets him he's a bargain.

You were sitting at your desk. You didn't turn round. You shook your head.

You *could*, I said, they positively *like* it if you talk about stuff like that at universities these days. There are whole courses, now, devoted to things like the Carry On films, or Coronation Street, or the changing orientation of Tom Cruise's hair in consecutive Mission: Impossible films.

That last one was true; I wasn't making it up. I actually had met a girl on a bus once who'd told me it was her PhD topic. I'd come home and told you and you'd laughed. Now it made you laugh again. Ten points to me.

Thanks, you said. I just want to concentrate, I just want to get these done.

You turned towards me, you looked pained. No, it wasn't pained you looked, it was *in* pain. You were pale with it.

You could so write about the marketplace in Oliver! I said. The Consider Yourself scene.

You waved me back with your hand.

You could write about Nancy singing As Long as

He Needs Me, I said. That's all about generosity. She's all about sacrifice. God, when you think about it, that whole film's about generosity and sacrifice.

Have you ever thought of reading the actual novel? you said.

I did, I said. Years ago.

You might like to read it again, you said. If you do, you'll find that there's not much singing, that Fagin's gang of boys is dark as can be, that Fagin's as close to talking about a child pornographer as a Victorian writer can come, and Dickens's sense of mercy, his generosity, is astonishing in the light of the dark he creates. And it's good about mirroring characters, Rose and Nancy, Oliver and the Dodger, Oliver and Dick—

Who's Dick? I said. There's no character called Dick in the film.

*Really* busy here, you said.

I could look up some of the lyrics for you, I said coming further into the room.

You held your hand up flat like a traffic policeman. With your other you covered the screen of your computer. You meant: get out.

Okay, I said. Call me if you need anything.

Now I had paused Oliver! on the dvd machine, Mark

Lester staring with astonishment at the barred window giving.

I looked out my own window. The sycamore was rude with opening buds. There were two young collared doves sitting close on a single branch.

I remembered something I'd read in that book I'd lifted from the charity shop in Brighton, about birds' eggs, how the egg of a bird is crystalline, made of layers lined with minuscule air canals so the chick inside can breathe; how the thickness of each egg's shell meets exactly the pressure each incubating bird will bring to bear on it.

Imagine me going into a shop and taking a book, taking two books and not paying. I must have been in a very bad way back then.

The collared doves out there were mates, they were doing a mating dance facing each other, pressed close to each other, mirroring each other's movements. Up went one head, up went the other. Down went one head, down went the other.

I left Oliver on freeze-frame, went through to the study desk. I moved my work records and the mess of envelopes I kept my accounts in; I shifted the old hard drive covered in dust. There they were, piled under it.

Maybe I hadn't read the last of them on purpose, so there'd still be something of yours I hadn't. Certainly I'd sorted and filed and decided about and thrown out and given away pretty much everything else by now. (That thought made me feel a bit better—charity shops had done very well out of us, I'd given them stuff of yours worth much much more than the couple of old books I'd taken.)

I peeled off the pages above On Time, the pages I'd not read yet, On Offer and On Reflection. I left the rest on the desk and went and sat under the anglepoise in the armchair I'd moved across the room last summer. Imagine, I'd actually felt bad about moving it, like I was being disloyal. But it was good here. See? It worked here.

Who was I talking to? Who was I telling all this to? Who cared what I did or didn't do, where I sat or didn't sit?

## 1. Putting the Art in Bartering

Offer: From the Latin, *ob*, towards, and *ferre*, to bring. To present as an act of devotion, homage, charity, etc. To express willingness. To hold out for acceptance or rejection. To lay before someone. To present to the mind. To propose to give, pay, sell, or perform. To attempt (violence, resistance, etc.). To make a show of attempting. To make as if. To give the enemy an opportunity for battle. To present itself. To be at hand. To incline or tend. To make an offer, i.e., of marriage. The act of offering. The state of being offered. Something which is offered. The first advance. A proposal made. An attempt or essay. A knob on an antler.

So offer involves rejection as well as acceptance. It involves everything between giving, selling, and merely thinking about either. It seems to be about both marriage and violence, and since an antler's involved—antlers being studded with offers—there'll probably be issues of both mating and territory. Offer means money, and the hope of money. There's an unanswered question at the heart of the word, the possibility of what *won't* materialize. In joinery, to offer something up means to position something loosely or unfixedly, to see whether it'll work before you fix it into place; in more usual usage, if you're offering something up, it's in the hope of persuading something to happen. So the notion of offer involves hope, a certain flexibility round acceptance or rejection, and the likelihood of both.

The notion of giving always involves, in multiple ways, the questions that surround taking. It's possible that where we recognize the generosity implicit in giving, we only much more rarely think about the generosity implicit in response to what's offered, in acceptance.

These are ancient terms, primal terms, as the poet HD suggests—aptly on several levels of consciousness here—in this story from her memoir, Tribute to Freud, about the problematics of giving a gift to her analyst, Sigmund Freud:

The Professor was seventy-seven. His birthday in May was significant. The consulting room in the strange house contained some of his treasures and his famous desk . . . Instead of the semicircle of priceless little *objets d'art*, there was a carefully arranged series of vases; each contained a spray of orchids or a single flower. I had nothing for the Professor. I said, 'I am sorry, I haven't brought you anything because I couldn't find what I wanted.' I said, 'Anyway, I wanted to give you something different.' My remark might have seemed a shade careless, a shade arrogant. It might have seemed either of these things, or both. I do not know how the Professor translated it. He waved me to the couch, satisfied or unsatisfied with my apparently casual regard for his birthday.

I had not found what I wanted so I did not give him anything. In one of our talks in the old room at Berggasse, we had gone off on one of our journeys . . . 'Ah, the Spanish Steps,' said the Professor . . . 'the gardenias! In Rome, even *I* could afford to wear a gardenia.'. . .

It was sometime later that the Professor received my gardenias . . . I found them in a West End florist's and scribbled on a card, 'To greet the return of the Gods.' The gardenias reached the Professor. I have his letter . . .

*Dear H.D., I got today some flowers. By chance or intention they are my favorite flowers, those I most admire. Some words 'to greet the return of the Gods' (other people read: Goods). No name. I suspect you to be responsible for the gift.*

Freud here, noting the slippage of others, marks exchange as a place where the gods and the goods come together. But the act of giving and accepting which goes between Freud and HD marks not just that crossover of matter and immortality, not just the act where authority is recognized and paid (or promised) homage, not just questions of satisfaction and its opposite, and not just the suggestion, fascinating in itself, that in some way we are (and will be held) responsible for what we give to others. It also includes these simple-seeming, repetitious statements: 'I haven't brought you anything because I couldn't find what I wanted,' and again a moment later, 'I had not found what I wanted so I did not give him anything.' In context, of course, it means HD simply hadn't found what she wanted to give Freud. But that's not what it very simply says. Very simply, it links the act of giving to that of fulfilling your own desire.

Giving frequently concerns—and addresses our concerns about—all we believe we have, and in terms that are much more than material. In The Golden Bowl, a novel about selfish and selfless loves and how human beings judge the worth of things, Henry James is keen to point up the dangerous resonances in all gift-giving. "Thank goodness then that if there *be* a crack, we know it!" Charlotte says when she finds out that the beautiful bowl she was about to buy as a wedding present, and which has been offered to her rather shadily as a 'bargain,' is worse than worthless. "But if we may perish by cracks in things that we don't know—!" And she smiled with the sadness of it. "We can never then give each other anything."

Giving is fraught with danger—as is taking. In Peter Hobbs's novel In the Orchard, the Swallows (2012), a young boy in Pakistan gives a girl socially divided from him by both gender and status a pomegranate from his father's beautiful orchard. She gives him her name. Gifts become the foundation of a narrative about the joint dangers and healing forces in generosity and hospitality, a story in which the boy, who ends up near-dead then imprisoned because of the unacceptability and the consequences of these gifts and this love, leaves jail a broken young man a decade later and is taken in off the street by a stranger who treats him as family. In this family, he learns to write. What he writes is the book we're holding in our hands, a gift of love for a girl who's unlikely ever to read it. The imagined giving and the act of art it involves become as important as the gift itself. The responsibility of accepting the gift radiates beyond the story's protagonists and passes to the reader of the novel.

Art is always an exchange, like love, whose giving and taking can be a complex and wounding matter, according to Michelangelo in this love sonnet (translated by Christopher Ryan): 'Within the sweetness of an immense kindness there often lurks concealed some offense to one's honor and one's life; . . . Anyone who gives wings to another's shoulders, and then along the way gradually spreads out a hidden net, extinguishes completely the ardent charity enkindled by love precisely where it most desires to burn.' It's interesting that the opposite happens, when it comes to wings, in Alexander Montgomerie's poem The Cherrie and the Slae, from the late 1500s, a work that's a near-contemporary of Michelangelo's sonnet. In it, Cupid, who's been woken by paradisal birdsong and feels like a bit of mischief, descends from the clouds and offers his wings, his bow, and his arrows to a man who's having a very nice time lying about listening to nature in an idyllic garden. The man, immediately taken with the golden wings, straps them onto his shoulders, rises into the sky, takes aim with one of the arrows and manages to shoot himself in the chest. He falls down through the air and hits the ground; Cupid holds his sides laughing and flies off, leaving the man bleeding and sorry for himself. But shooting himself with Cupid's arrow has kindled a different, unexpected gift in the man. The narcissistic wound in his chest starts to glow with courage and desire the like of which he's never felt.

In Paradise you're bound to be offered all sorts of

fruits, all sorts of free advice from snakes, which you'll end up paying dearly for. There's a short story by Tove Jansson, one of her earliest pieces written specifically for adults rather than children, which suggests that maybe all offering (and by extension the profanation we call art) is about the gulf between human and divine, and about getting some kind of attention from God, at least getting some kind of dialogue going. In this story (translated by Kingsley Hart), two small cousins are playing a game called the Children of Israel in a field behind their grandparents' idyllic house:

We raised our voices in the wilderness and were continually disobedient because God so likes to forgive sinners. God forbade us to gather manna under the laburnum tree but we did all the same. Then he sent worms up from the earth to eat up the manna. But we went on being disobedient and we still raised our voices.

All the time we expected him to get so angry that he would show himself. The very idea was tremendous. We could think of nothing but God. We sacrificed to him, we gave him blueberries and crab apples and flowers and milk and sometimes we made a small burnt-offering. We sang for him and we prayed to him to give us a sign that he was interested in what we were doing.

One morning Karin said that the sign had come to her. He had sent a yellow bunting into her room and it had perched on the picture of Jesus Walking on the Waters and nodded its head three times.

Verily, verily I say unto you, Karin said, many are called but few are chosen.

She put on a white dress and went round all day with roses in her hair and sang hymns and carried on in a very affected way.

The story becomes an examination of the place where art meets both profanation and offering. As one child grows holier-than-thou and starts holding Bible classes in the field for all the cousins staying with the grandparents for the summer, 'even the ones who couldn't talk yet,' the other goes to the most pagan place she can find in the garden, a dark spruce-lined tree circle. There she does the worst thing she can imagine. 'It was then I made the golden calf':

It was very difficult to get the legs to stay upright but in the end they did . . . Sometimes I stood still, listening for the first rumble of the wrath of God. But so far he had said nothing. His great eye just looked down into the arbor through the hole between the tops of the spruce trees. At last I had got him to show some interest . . . God kept completely quiet. Perhaps he was waiting for me to take out the matches. He wanted to see if I really would do something so awful as to sacrifice to the golden calf and, even worse, dance in front of it afterwards. Then he would come down from his hill in a cloud of lightning and wrath and show that he knew that I existed . . . I stood there and listened and listened and the silence grew and grew until it was overpowering. Everything was listening.

Offering and sacrifice are at one level a direct request for dialogue, and at another ask the existential question—not so much do You exist, as do I?

EE Cummings is in no doubt about the answer in this sonnet:

i thank You God for most this amazing
day:for the leaping greenly spirits of trees
and a blue true dream of sky;and for everything
which is natural which is infinite which is yes

(i who have died am alive again today,
and this is the sun's birthday;this is the birth
day of life and of love and wings:and of the gay
great happening illimitably earth)

how should tasting touching hearing seeing
breathing any—lifted from the no
of all nothing—human merely being
doubt unimaginable You?

(now the ears of my ears awake and
now the eyes of my eyes are opened)

Who's he talking to, really? Who's he persuading? The poem is an offering of thanks for the fact that every rhetorical question is its own completed dialogue; it carries its own answer. There's a loving, curmudgeonly, late poem of Auden's called Talking to Myself, in which the speaker addresses, throughout, a You with a capital y; this is its last verse:

Time, we both know, will decay You, and already
I'm scared of our divorce: I've seen some horrid ones.
Remember: when *Le Bon Dieu* says to You *Leave him!*,

please, please, for His sake and mine, pay no attention
to my piteous *Don't*'s, but bugger off quickly.

Cummings, of course, will never die, that's what he's persuading us of in his sonnet, and persuading his capital
You about; it's a multiple birthday in his sonnet. The
crux of Cummings's offering is the statement of rebirth:
'i who have died am alive again today.' For only gods
and Gods, traditionally, can grant immortality. Careful,
though, for the gods can take as well as give and they
have a habit of giving complicated gifts, like shirts which
stick to the skin so you can't get them off without skin-
ning yourself into the bargain, or showers of coins which
leave you pregnant by Zeus and get you and your new son
thrown into the sea locked in a wooden trunk by your
father for defying him, as in the myth of Danaë and
Perseus. It's possible that the gift of wings, one way or
another, always involves the net Michelangelo warned
us of. But certainly gifts tend to breed gifts—that's what
exchange is—and with any godly luck an old fisherman
will catch the wooden trunk in his net, open it up and
free the pair to carry on with the story.

And, give or take a bit of give and take, it's always all

about continuance. This is Colette, from The Pure and the Impure (translated by Herma Briffault): 'Amalia X, that good comic actress of road companies who died at the beginning of the war . . . if one were to believe her, had not hesitated to leave a sleeping and satiated sultan and go on foot, veiled, through the night streets of Constantinople to a hotel room where a sweet, blonde, and very young woman was waiting up for her . . .' In this anecdote Colette sums up almost casually (though Colette wrote nothing without deliberation, without performative poise) the ways that giving the self and telling a good story might not just be related to each other but both have roots in notions of belief, or suspension thereof.

Has giving, since the first gift of the apple, always been a matter involving purity, impurity, issues of permissibility? Here's a slightly more contemporary French story, from Philippe Lioret's 2009 film, Welcome, where a young Kurdish illegal immigrant from Iraq, trying to reach his girlfriend in London, gets himself as far as Calais. Twenty-one miles of Channel divide him and his destination, with no way he can smuggle himself in. So he starts taking swimming lessons locally. His French swimming instructor befriends him. The friendship is as illegal as inviting an illegal immigrant into your home is, in Calais, in the year 2009. We are living in times where, very close to home, hospitality is punishable by law.

Boris Pasternak, via his translator Edwin Morgan in the poem The Wedding Party, sees giving the self as the way in which we wed the world, the way we simultaneously free ourselves and commit ourselves:

Life is only a moment, life too is only a dissolving
of ourselves in all others as by an act of giving:

only a wedding's gladness thrilling up through a window,
only a song, only a sleep, only a slate-gray pigeon.

Casanova puts it this way: 'the greatest exhilaration to my spirits, greater than all my own pleasure, was the joy of giving pleasure to a woman.' EM Forster, though, saw it a little more evenhandedly: 'when human beings love they try to get something. They also try to give something, and this double aim makes love more complicated than food or sleep. It is selfish and altruistic at the same time, and no amount of specialization in one direction quite atrophies the other.'

Forster's vision of love here, a combination of generosity and canniness, sounds like what Jan Verwoert thinks of the nature of all offerings in his recent article about the ethics of profanity. Referring to Giorgio Agamben's 2007 essay In Praise of Profanity, he says:

> in antiquity, ritual sacrifice would entail a portion of the sacrificial gift to the gods (e.g., parts of an animal) being returned to the community as a profane share (e.g., free food) to be enjoyed by all, as an earthly thing which retained a trace of the divine. (It's like true irreverence, which always has love at the heart of it.) So value resides neither in the divine nor the profane but is manifested in the dynamic relation between the two. Capitalist society, Agamben argues, nullifies this dynamic. When there is a price on everything, all is similarly worthy and worthless. The challenge is to revive the free interplay between profanation and veneration through anarchic practices that affect the motion and emotion of meaningful differences coming into being.

The challenge is to understand the real meaning and worth of all that glisters, golden calf, golden bowl. But the line of Verwoert's that tickles most here (a throwaway

irreverent line, in parentheses) is the one about true irreverence always having love at its heart.

In Colette's story, it's apt that the pure/impure lover-
and-giver crossing the city in the night, dead at the start
of the story then brought to rich, luxuriant life by Colette
choosing to tell it, is a 'good comic actress of road companies' (NB too, to tell is also a verb that means to count,
particularly to count coins; that's why bank tellers are
called tellers). The comic form and concepts of anarchy,
irreverence, luxury, rags-to-riches, are connected to concepts of generosity and transformation.

The resolving force of coincidence, the generosity in
the workings of Dickens's plots, comes straight down the
line from Shakespeare's comedies, backed by the source
of Shakespeare's most powerful forms of magic and
coincidence in his late plays, Cymbeline, The Winter's
Tale, The Tempest, plays that fuse category to defy category, where tragedy and comedy coexist, fight it out, re-
solve in forms of uncanny rebirth, findings of those who
were lost and restorings of the dead to life, usually via a
display of working artifice.

Shakespeare's late plays love and exalt the poor, whose
comic literary ethos, over the centuries, takes the form of
sharing, inclusion, and hospitality, from the taking in

and rescuing of the abandoned baby in The Winter's Tale to the taking in and bringing up to lives of comic thievery of lost boys which forms the employment of the markedly much more comic creation of Fagin in Lionel Bart's 1960s stage musical.

In Carol Reed's 1968 film version of this musical, Fagin is played by Ron Moody as practically benign, a much more generous, much less threatening and doomed creation than Dickens's original, in a London whose comic commoner ethos, so long as 'nobody tries to be lah-de-dah or uppity,' is that 'there's a cup o' tea for all,' a twentieth-century mockney first cousin to the cup o' kindness Robert Burns proffers in Auld Lang Syne, the song where old friends, long parted, promise hospitality to each other infinitely. Auld Lang Syne is the closest thing to a worldwide ritual of well-wishing we have—a New Year song that holds the worth of the past and all kind hopes for the future in the exchange of hands. The word kindred and the word kind are related; the words for kindness and family have etymology in common.

'O wad some Pow'r the giftie gie us / To see oursels as others see us!' That's Burns too, in To a Louse, a satire addressed to a louse making its way across the bonnet of a lady in a church, a lady who thinks herself finer than she is, in a world where riches and rags are both a kind of fodder. Arguably some mischievous god heard Burns and granted this wish to our culture: blessed, we are, with the gifts of celebrity, surveillance, and reality tv. O wad some Pow'r the giftie gie us to act like Chaplin, irreverent, anarchic, empathetic, the most world-famous and the richest by far of the comic actors of road companies. No stranger to poverty, he played it playfully, as a state in which real richness is having finesse, delicacy, and generosity when you have nothing else; typically, as David Robinson records in his critical biography, looking out of a window with his two small sons, Chaplin 'would train a telescope on some far-off pedestrian' and tell them, 'You see that man? He must be going home after a day's work. Look at his gait, so slow, so tired. His head's bent. Something's on his mind. What could it be!'

This is part empathy, part thievery. Empathy, in art, is art's part-exchange with us, its inclusivity, at once a kindness, a going beyond the self, and a pickpocketing of our responses, which is why giving and taking are bound up with the goods, with the gods, with respect, with deep-seated understanding about the complex cultural place where kindness, thievery, bartering, and gift-giving all meet, make their exchanges, and by exchange reveal real worth. We are what we give. 'To give, it is a witty thing,' Ovid says, via Christopher Marlowe's translation of Elegies of Love. Actually Marlowe's whole line is: '(Trust me) to give, it is a witty thing.' Exchange *is* dialogue (and that includes the exchange between Ovid and Marlowe, the dialogue that the translation represents). But more—in this single line the verb *to give* is held between two opposing notions. Being *a witty thing*, giving is about knowledge, about knowing (these are some of the synonyms for wit). But before you even get to giving, something must be taken—on *trust*—and this is where the exchange becomes to do with an act of faith in something beyond *you*. *(Trust me.)*

## 2. Hello my darling, how are you? I hope you are very well, are you?

I sat up. I read that title over again.

Hello my darling, how are you? I hope you are very well, are you?

Below it, you had typed up the following, in a slightly smaller size of typeface like you did when you were quoting someone, and as if it were part of your talk.

I mean, seriously, what are the chances of you ever reading this essay? ha, essay happens to be one of the words I found in Chambers Dictionary when I looked up offer, next to the word attempt. Attempt, essay, offering. If you ARE reading these offerings, remember, they're just attempts. You know I can't do argument (apart from with you, I mean—we do have some really good arguments, I'm quite proud of some of *them*).

Anyway a minute ago you were in here trying to persuade me to write about Oliver the musical. See above. I've quoted Consider yourself and have riffed it in (in a critically really unproven way, may God forgive me) with Shakespeare and Burns especially for you, will that do?

One of the reasons I'm writing this is that I was rather harsh with you just now. I'm sorry.

It's actually because you nearly caught me.

You don't know. You think I'm in here working really hard and listening to Beethoven on the headphones, when I'm actually sitting looking online— Not looking up porn (though I have done, and it's interesting to; an awful lot of take and not much give, not much edge, pretty standardized form, and, from what I can see, bloody well endless)—no, I'm watching a blonde girl singing and dancing in countless bright 60s film sets.

What—a sea-change? no, I'd never be able to get that much distance on my true character this late in life, no, it all started because I was thinking about Antigone, the girl from Sophocles's Theban Plays who tried to bury her dead brother, but her dead brother had been declared a traitor, so her uncle the king, who'd ruled this burial against the law, condemned Antigone to death for breaking it, then decided he'd bury her alive instead, put her in a cave and wall up the mouth, a death that wouldn't look quite so bad to the populace. I was trying to remember a quote, I can't find it, I don't know whether it's in one of the Sophocles translations or Anouilh wrote it or Brecht or maybe it's in Heaney's version, or maybe I've even just made it up. But what I think I remember her saying is something like: being alive is nothing, it's trivial, compared to all the not-being-alive we did before we were born and the not-being-alive we'll do after we're dead.

And for some reason that made me think about the woman Colette describes, Amalia X, that good comic actress of road companies, and I found myself hoping it was true, hoping it really happened, the journey between the lovers that she takes.

Then I wondered if Amalia X, who I'm not even sure existed, ever found herself playing Antigone.

For some reason I was sitting here furious with longing for her to have played *all* the parts, *all* the comic and the tragic and the Imogens and the Hermiones, I wanted her to be Hermione and Perdita at once, then I wanted her to be Prospero too. I was suddenly in love with her versatility, full of energy from imagining it.

Then I began to wonder if there was an actress alive now who was versatile enough to be Amalia X *and* Antigone, to play all the parts, the highs and the lows, the Consider yourself songs *and* the being-walled-up-till-everybody-kills-themselves, so I typed into the Google search box three or four things all together one after the other to see what would happen, I typed in *Antigone* first, then off the top of my head the names of a bunch of musicals with strong female leads, *Evita Sound of Music Cabaret*, and I pressed search.

What happened next is unbelievable: it actually

came up with someone. The first thing on the screen was the name of a Greek woman (dead now, she died in the mid-90s) who played ALL FOUR in her time, Antigone, Evita, that mad pure Julie Andrews nun with the guitar, and the gorgeous debauched Sally Bowles—as well as Shirley Valentine and Shaw's Pygmalion and Aristophanes's Lysistrata and the leads in My Fair Lady and in Tennessee Williams's Sweet Bird of Youth, and dressed up as a boy in a Greek film musical version of Romeo and Juliet, and more. There's one film in which she seems to be playing herself as twins, one is rich, living in a chic uptown apartment, and one is poor, living hand to mouth in a hovel, selling combs on the street and avoiding the police. One gets mistaken for the other, of course, like in Shakespeare, and Twain. The poor one looks a bit like your Nancy from the Oliver film, and at one point, like her, she sings a song in a room full of lost boys—except the poverty round her actually looks a lot like realism.

Anyway she was apparently a legend in Greek cinema and theater from the 50s all through the 60s and 70s, into the 80s, even the 90s, all through the huge changes in Greek politics, she was the Greek Monroe, Bardot, Loren, Hepburn (Katharine *and* Audrey), and she seems to have been like all of them rolled into one, and had a kind of Greek pastry and a doll both named after her, and had a kind of Elizabeth Taylor/ Richard Burton relationship with her leading man, and almost with a Greek prince too at one point, I gather.

Out of curiosity I watched a few clips from some films.

What I knew immediately was how much you would really love these films.

So here's a small present for the future from the past, from me to you with love. A lot of it is in Greek but if you type this in she'll come up singing: Aliki Vougiouklaki.

I can just see you watching these. It gives me such pleasure to imagine it. & to imagine you imagining me here in the evenings, deep in some piano concerto, and me actually watching bits of old Greek musical from the 1960s ha ha! that gives me even more pleasure. Like we've swapped sides of the mirror. Aliki by the way is Greek for Alice.

When you came in just now, what I was doing was watching a bit from a film called Modern Cinderella (I think), about a girl who's so poor she can't even afford a bottle of milk, but then by chance and by cleverness she gets a really good job and the first thing she does is phone up the grocer she owes money to, pay her bill, and order all the groceries her family hasn't been able to have for weeks—better than that, she orders the best things the man has in his shop, and the next scene is her whole neighborhood at a party, that's what I was watching. She sings a song, it's called (in Greeklish) Ypomoni.

Just a passing thought, to apologize if I seemed or seem harsh, I'm really sorry, and to explain why I didn't want you to see the screen—i.e., I wasn't really working, and I was suddenly unbelievably embarrassed in case you found out I wasn't, and even worse, that instead of working I was trawling the net for things you'd love.

I'm sorry if I seem impatient. I am impatient. If I were more patient I'd sit and work this into the talk— importance of clowning, what characters do with what they're given, empathy of observer, gift at heart of transformation story, clowns in Shakespeare, Josephine Baker and her use of comic mask, but what the fuck. Talking of what the fuck, I thought of you when I was writing about Freud's flowers. And there was a quote from a Michael Ondaatje novel I wrote down and was keeping for this talk and haven't used, but it really makes me think of us, well, makes me think of you. 'She had an eager spirit. One mentioned a possibility and she met it, like the next line of a song.'

Wherever you are all the trees above your head are flowering.

You're next door right now.


I read your letter I don't know how many times.

I poured myself a whiskey. I drank it. I poured myself another. I went through and got my laptop and typed into the search box the words *Ypomoni aliki vougiouklaki*.

It wasn't very good quality. But up came a black and white table loaded with food, wine, beer, then the camera revealed both sides of the table crammed with people, and at the end, at the head of it, were some musicians and a woman with very bright hair.

I clicked about a bit to find a better version, one not so pixelated.

The woman with the bright hair was holding a party, being hospitable, smiling, helping the people next to her at the table to food. She had dark eyes but she sat like a torch lit at the end of the long table and when the camera came up close to her like she was irresistible and it couldn't not, she was singing along with the man next to her who was playing a mandolin thing (later I'd find out it's called a bouzouki). Then she raised a glass to the whole table: cheers! she said, I think, in Greek, and everybody at the table said it straight back in response.

I looked up some other clips featuring this actress. In one, in blazing color, she was on the back of a donkey in a procession of people on donkeys coming down the slope of a hill through countryside below sky, rich blues and greens, and she sang a happy-sounding song all the way to the sea. In another she did a dance that made me laugh out loud, because she was such a rubbish dancer. A couple of clips later I realized that this actress had made a grace out of being a rubbish dancer, that whenever she danced in a film she did it like a human being, like someone who's only quite good. In fact, everything she did had something both graceful and a bit gauche about it— gauche like a real person, not an actress being gauche— the way she moved her body, flicked her nose, blew her hair out of her eyes, squared herself for her next line of song or dialogue. She was charming, especially in the early footage. She was camp in a way that was innocent of sarcasm. She was passionate and funny both at once, like she could play them simultaneously because they were really the same thing. In one clip she danced round a big hanging fishing net in a restaurant then round a table in the restaurant and her skirt knocked a basket of bread off the table, and I couldn't tell whether that was supposed to happen in the film or had happened spontaneously in the take and they'd kept it in because it was so right.

At three in the morning on the first night of longer spring light of the year, I took your pages on offer and reflection to bed with me and I read your letter again.

To be known so well by someone is an unimaginable gift. But to be imagined so well by someone is even better.

I sat up in bed and read what you'd written about reflection.

When I thought it was probably time I got off to sleep, the new day's light was up.

## 1. Through the Looking

If art is a holding up of the mirror to nature, then The Mirror of Ink, the short story by Jorge Luis Borges (translated by María Kodama), teaches us that the vision which comes from nature united with art—the magic vision of the world in all its facets, there in the pool of ink in the palms of our own hands—is almost unbearably beautiful and will mesmerize us with this beauty, then with revelations of our cruelty and mortality. 'He was possessed by the mirror; he did not even try to turn his eyes aside, or to spill out the ink.'

Angela Carter's early novels are full of troubled and broken mirrors, blinding narcissisms and deceptions, distorting halls-of-mirrors reflecting desire as a mirror-show which begins as exoticism and ends in violence and violation—in the rape experienced, for example, by Desiderio, the protagonist in The Infernal Desire Machines of Doctor Hoffman (1972), at the hands (and the eyes) of the Acrobats of Desire, in their 'metallic shifts' which 'wounded the retina.' The insides of the Acrobats' traveling-van is walled with mirrors and photographs. 'Had I not known all along it was done with mirrors?' he says, before the Acrobats literally 'do' him:

the men were infinitely repeated everywhere I looked and now eighteen and sometimes twenty-seven and, at one time thirty-six brilliant eyes were fixed on me. . . . I was Saint Sebastian stuck through with the visible barbed beams from brown, translucent eyes which spun a web of fine, shining threads on the air like strands of candified sugar. Once again they juggled with their hypnotic eyes and used their palpable eye strings to bind me in invisible bonds.

But in her final novel, Wise Children (1991), Carter resolves the fracturing, the cultural deceptions and vanities which up to now she has associated with mirror-imaging, in her creation of Dora and Nora Chance, a pair of twins born on the wrong side of the tracks, mirrors to each other and a mirror, too, to their own far side, the upper-class family to which they illegitimately belong. The novel is an act of synthesis performed by talented hoofers whose syncopation brings together, into the same dance, the opposing forces: youth and age, wealth and poverty, theater and cinema, high art and low, Shakespeare and music hall, plus this reflective healing act tossed back over their shoulders at all the divided or violated Carter selves who came before them.

Here's a story from Oscar Wilde about what happens when reflection is at its most narcissistic:

When Narcissus died, the flowers of the field were desolate and asked the river for some drops of water to weep for him. 'Oh!' answered the river, 'if all my drops of water were tears, I should not have enough to weep for Narcissus myself. I love him.' 'Oh!' replied the flowers of the field, 'how could you not have loved Narcissus? He was beautiful.' 'Was he beautiful?' said the river. 'And who should know better than you? Each day, leaning over your bank, he beheld his beauty in your waters.' 'If I loved him,' replied the river, 'it was because, when he leaned over my waters, I saw the reflection of my waters in his eyes.'

By contrast, here's Margaret Atwood on the place where reflection meets art and artfulness:

The act of writing takes place at the moment when Alice passes through the mirror. At this one instant, the glass barrier between the doubles dissolves, and Alice is neither here nor there, neither art nor life, neither the one thing nor the other, though at the same time she is all of these at once. At that moment time itself stops, and also stretches out, and both writer and reader have all the time not in the world.

All reflection involves both Narcissus and Hermes. EM Forster, in Aspects of the Novel, reminds his readers that 'a mirror does not develop because a historical pageant passes in front of it. It only develops when it gets a fresh coat of quicksilver—in other words, when it acquires new sensitiveness.' Quicksilver is another word for Mercury, is another word for a planet that looks like a gray boulder in space, is another word for an element which is both fluid and solid, can change its shape yet still hold its form, is another word for Hermes, Greek god of art, artfulness, thievery, changeability, swiftness of thought and of communication, language, the alphabet, speechmaking, emails, texts, tweets; god of bartering, trade, liaison, roads and crossroads, travelers, the stock exchange, wages, dreams; guide between the surface world and the underworld, guide between the living and the dead, stealer of unbreakable nets for catching pretty virgins, god of free association, god of freedom of movement, fluidity, mutability of form, broad-hatted heel-winged god of all going-between, the deliverer. Another word for delivery? Birth.

What's the first thing the god Hermes did on the day of his own birth? This is how Ciaran Carson tells it, in Fishing for Amber:

Born in the morning . . . by midday Hermes had invented the lyre. Getting up from his cradle, he ventured out and found a tortoise. He killed it and scooped out the flesh. Then he found a goat and beheaded it. He put the curved horns of the goat through the front leg-holes of the tortoise-shell, and he made strings of the goat's guts.

The next thing he does is steal—his first theft is a herd of cows, from Apollo. Apollo catches him, and while they're arguing about the cows, Hermes starts strumming the lyre. That's nice, Apollo says. If I can have that thing you've made, we'll forget about the cattle, they're yours.

God of quick-wittedness, god of the musical potential of the shells of dead things, god of getting a tune out of goat-guts, but above all god of perfect timing, god of canny slippage, god of changing the subject. Lavinia Greenlaw, in this poem called The Messenger God, sees Mercury, Hermes, as god of response and responsiveness:

How do you know?
He is ahead and to the quick.

What impression?
Grave, fissile.

Easily divided?
In that he responds.

His message?
His presence. No other message.

To what purpose?
Glass in a city of water and sky.

What need of him?
I must enter the city.

To what purpose?
Water and sky.

In this series of ritualized, gnomic questions and responses, Greenlaw discusses the nature of how we know
anything. Because of this messenger going ahead of us,
whose quickness is a reminder that alive and very fast
both sometimes mean the same thing, we are able not
just to know but to see where we are and where we're liv-

ing. With this mercurial god, division comes to mean response. His presence allows transparency, protection, a seeing through something *and* an act of seeing something through.

At one level reflection means we see ourselves. At another, it's another word for the thought process. We can choose to use it to look into the light of our own eyes, or we can be light sensitive, we can allow all things to move over and through us; we can hold them and release them, in thought. Broken things become pattern in reflection. The way a kaleidoscope works is to allow fragmentary or disconnected things to become their own harmony. Cross an artist with a fighter plane and—as with Fiona Banner's Jaguar (2010), her sculpture installation of a burnished Sepecat Jaguar fighter aircraft on the floor on its side—you'll get an unexpected reflective surface. It's one you can see yourself in—or rather, one placed so that you can't *not* see a version of yourself in it; a reminder of what weaponry is, what it means in real terms, and what humankind is, what it means in real terms.

Here's to the 'wreathed trellis of a working brain': that's what Keats called it in Ode to Psyche. Here's to what George Mackay Brown said about how he spent his days: 'I assure you, there are few jobs in life like the leafing and blossoming of the imagination.' Here's to what Clarice Lispector (in her 1977 novel, The Hour of the Star, translated by Giovanni Pontiero) said: 'So long as I have questions to which there are no answers, I shall go on writing.' Here's to what Edwin Morgan said: 'Forget your literature?—forget your soul.' He said this in a poem called Retrieving and Renewing. Here's to what David Constantine said in his work on why the arts matter: 'no society that I know of has done without poetry, which must mean it can't be done away with (some have tried) or done without.' Here's to this poem by Paul Eluard, translated by Stuart Kendall, about the nature of story-telling, or of all telling:

I told you for the clouds
I told you for the sea tree
for each wave for the birds in the leaves
for pebbles of noise
for the familiar hands
for the eye that becomes a face or a landscape
and the sleep that renders the sky from its color
for the entire drunken night
for the grid of the roads

for the open window for an uncovered face
I told you for your thoughts for your words
every caress every confidence endures

Here's to the place where reality and the imagination meet, whose exchange, whose dialogue, allows us not just to imagine an unreal different world but also a real different world—to match reality with possibili

That's as far as you got. That was it over.

I'd read all of you, now.

And now the hand that traces these words, falters, as it approaches the conclusion of its task; and would weave, for a little longer space, the thread of these adventures.

I woke up at about eleven the next morning. When I came downstairs, Oliver! was still on freeze-frame. The screen had been glowing that same picture, of the moment the window in the undertaker's cellar opens in the snow, out into the living room all night.

I switched it off. I got my new copy of Oliver Twist down off the shelf. (I had a new copy now, I'd shelved it next to the old fallen-apart copy. I hadn't actually opened the new copy yet.) I'd decided, last night, as I was falling asleep, that I'd finally finish that novel, that when I woke up it would be the first thing I'd do.

The first thing I noticed when I flicked the brand-new copy open was the word Mudfog. It was in the very first line, the word. It was the name of the place Oliver was born. But in my other copy Dickens had made a point of *not* mentioning the name of the place that Oliver was born. I remembered that from starting this book last summer—all those months ago.

Mudfog. I went and got my old falling-apart copy off the shelf to check. 'Among other public buildings in the town of Mudfog.' 'Among other public places in a certain town which for many reasons it will be prudent to refrain from mentioning.' I held the old copy in one hand and the newer copy in the other and I laughed. It was as though there was an argument, a discussion, literally happening between the copies, like the book itself, Oliver Twist, was weighing up and still undecided about the things it was going to say.

I made coffee. I phoned up work and told them I'd overslept. They put me straight through to Sandra. I got reprimanded quite sharply down the phone then congratulated on being honest enough not to make up a cold or a flu.

Come in by 2 pm and I'll pretend it didn't happen, she said.

Can I come in after I've finished Oliver Twist? I said.

After *what*? she said. Now you're really pushing your luck. No you can't. Come in right now.

Oh. Okay, I said.

There was a pause.

Well how many pages exactly have you got to go? she said.

Not much, I said. Twenty pages. Thirty. Well, thirty-seven.

It's good, Oliver Twist, she said. Okay, but be in here as soon as you're done.

When I came off the phone to work, I went online (really quickly) and looked up some local language schools. I wrote an email to one and asked did they teach basic Greek and could they teach someone like me from scratch. They wrote back very fast and very keenly. I suppose in this recession not very many people are taking language classes or thinking about learning new languages.

Soon I'd know a new alphabet; soon, working from a book meant for five-year-olds, I'd be learning how to say some very simple sentences. Concurrently I'd also be learning a whole other kind of Greek since my teacher would turn out to be an Aliki Vougiouklaki fan, having grown up with her films like I grew up with Oliver!, and would use songs from these films to teach me as well as this basic grammar book, which meant that soon, along with the verbs for to have and to want, along with sentences like *I have a book*, *I have a pencil*, *I want a notebook*, I'd know the words for *unkissed boy* and be able to say things like *the swallows have written it on the skies*, *for the first time*, *my heart is shining inside me* and *a lemon tree will bloom in the neighborhood*. That last line, about the lemon tree, is from the song called Ypomoni, or Patience, it's written by Stavros Xarhakos and Alekos Sakellarios, and, roughly translated (by me myself actually), it goes:

Neighborhood, your streets are narrow
Frost and gray skies

Life is dark, day and night
For company, cloudy skies

Patience.

Have patience and the sky will become more
  blue
Have patience: a lemon tree will bloom in the
  neighborhood.

But that wouldn't be till the summer. For now, this lunchtime, with all the birds in the trees mad with spring outside, I poured my coffee into the favorite mug, came through to the study, curled myself into the armchair and I read to the end.

Then I went back nearly a hundred pages and read again the bit where the Artful is in court and how after his trial he leaves the courtroom 'establishing for himself a glorious reputation' as he goes; ironic, of course, and at the same time completely true. In fact, glorious reputation is the last we hear of him.

You know what I really like? I said out loud in the empty room. It's how Dickens, when he sums up near the very end of the book what's happened to all the people in the gang, well, in the whole book, when he lists the characters one after the other and tells us what became of them, he never directly mentions the Dodger. It's like the Dodger's given not just the story the slip, but given Dickens the slip too.

(Who did I think I was talking to?

You.)

*Oliver plucks up a Spirit*

The perfect form, the beautifull fac
elegant manners of Lucy so won on
e affections of Alice that when they
arted, which was not till after Supper
he afsured her that except her Fathe
rothers, Uncles, Aunts, Cousins & other
elations, Lady Williams, Charles adan
a few dozen more of particular frien
he loved her better than almost any
ther person in the world.

Such a flattering afsurance of
er regard would justly have given muc
leasure to the object of it, had she not
lainly perceived that the amiable Ali
ad partaken too freely of Lady Williams's
laret.

Her Ladyship (whose discernmen

S. Vere Benson

# BIRDS AT SIGHT

## HOW TO KNOW THEM

CHARACTERS from CHARLES DICKENS.

"THE ARTFUL DODGER."
( Oliver Twist )

"If you don't take pocket handkerchers
and watches, some other cove
will, so that the coves that lose
'em will be all the worse, and
you'll be all the worse too,
and nobody half a ha'porth
the better, except the chap
wot gets them."

Kyd.

CHARA

A paro
and
bu
as
s

K

CHARACTERS from CHARLES DICKENS.

"MR. MICAWBER."
( David Copperfield )

I am, however delighted
to add that I have now
an immediate prospect of
something turning up.

CHARACTERS

"Widd
WIII

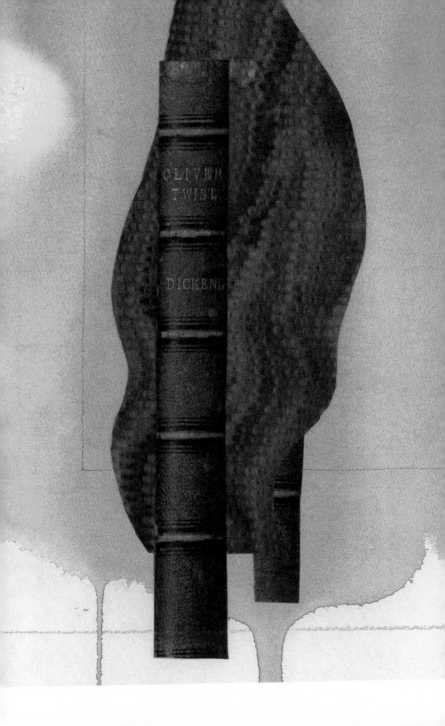

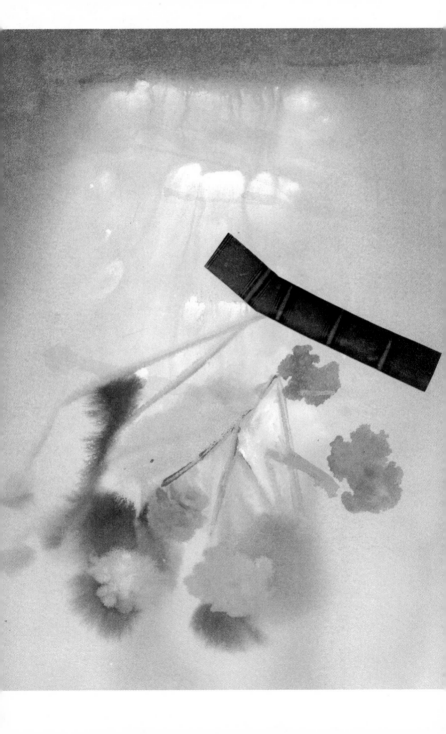

# Some sources used in the writing of these talks

The epigraph is from the Song of the Flow of Things in Bertolt Brecht's Man Equals Man (1926).

## On time

Angela Carter resees Blake's Tyger as a pajama case in her 1978 essay, Little Lamb Get Lost; George Mackay Brown imagined the land of Tir-Nan-Og in midsummer of 1981 in one of his newspaper columns for the Orcadian, collected in the 1992 volume, Rockpools and Daffodils; Walter Benjamin writes about the storyteller's authority in his 1936 essay, The Storyteller; the quote from Margaret Atwood about time comes from her 2002 book of lecture-essays, Negotiating with the Dead: A Writer on Writing; all the Shakespeare references here to Time with a capital T come from the sonnets, and the two lines quoted in full are from Sonnet 64. The letter by Katherine Mansfield is dated 1909, to an unidentified recipient; in it she is worrying about the strange and changeable nature of her heart. Michelangelo's urgent instructions to his assistant, Antonio Mini, can be found on a Virgin and Child sketch held in the British Museum; the Montale/Morgan translation comes from the poem called Brief Testament; Three Wheels on My Wagon was written by Bob Hilliard to music by Burt Bacharach in 1961 and was a hit for the New Christy Minstrels in 1962; the quote from Victor Klemperer comes from the volume of his diaries entitled The Lesser Evil; and Jackie Kay kindly wrote http://www.google.co.uk especially for these talks.

## On form

begins with a poem made of lines from famous poems by, consecutively, Wallace Stevens, Emily Dickinson,

William Blake, Samuel Taylor Coleridge, Stevie Smith, John Keats, Dylan Thomas, WB Yeats, Sylvia Plath, WH Auden, Edward Thomas, and Philip Larkin. Ted Hughes meets Ovid in Hughes's 1997 collection, Tales from Ovid; the Graham Greene comment on Shakespeare's Troilus and Cressida comes from Shirley Hazzard's book Greene on Capri (2000); its original source is an essay on British dramatists which Greene wrote in the 1940s. Later in this chapter I quote again from this memoir (whose slimness belies its richness), from a conversation Hazzard had with Greene about the impression reading War and Peace made on him. Thom Gunn's definition of poetry comes from My Life up to Now, the autobiographical introduction to his bibliography in 1979; this can also be found in his collection of essays, The Occasions of Poetry (1982). It's Kasia Boddy, decades ago, who drew my attention with her usual unique, generous, and fruitful eclecticism to the confluence of Shakespeare and Stevens in Morgan's Not Marble; the Horace reference comes from the Odes, III.30; Woolf's quote about the born writer and the husks of words comes from her essay on Oliver Goldsmith; the heart as metaphor, or not, comes from Elizabeth Hardwick's 1979 novel Sleepless Nights. I've purposefully misquoted the line from the song Smile, for which Charlie Chaplin wrote the tune (it was music that featured in his 1936 film, Modern Times); the true first line is slightly different, though I'd bet it's more often remembered as this misquote. The lyrics for Chaplin's piece of music were written by John Turner and Geoffrey Parsons nearly twenty years after Chaplin composed it. The lines about the singing bird and the apple-tree are from Christina Rossetti's poem A Birthday; the Ovid references a paragraph later come from the stories of Apollo and Daphne and Philemon and Baucis, in Metamorphoses; the quotations from Pound come from his poem The Tree, and from New Age, January 7, 1915; the lines about the star-eaten blanket of the sky come from the poem The Embankment, by TE Hulme. This is Katherine Mansfield on the hotel's-worth of selves: 'True to oneself! Which self? Which of my many—well, really, that's what it looks like coming to—hundreds of selves. For what with complexes and suppressions, and reactions and vibrations and reflections—there are moments when I feel I am nothing but the small clerk of some hotel without a proprietor who has all his work cut out to enter the names and hand the keys to the willful guests' (The Katherine Mansfield Notebooks, Vol. II, ed. Margaret Scott, University of Minnesota Press, 2002). The quote from Woolf is from the last pages of A Room of One's Own; the one from Yayoi Kusama, translated here by Ralph McCarthy, comes from her 2002 autobiography, Infinity Net. The quotations from Italo Calvino are from Six Memos for the Next Millennium, translated here by Patrick Creagh; these stories about Cézanne—and many more—can be found in Paul Cézanne: His Life and Art by Ambroise Vollard, which I read in the translation by Harold L. Van Doren published in 1924; and it's the character of the Beadle, Mr. Bumble, who lays claim to naming Oliver Twist alphabetically.

## On edge

The quote from Leonora Carrington comes from a story called The Stone Door, written in the 1940s. Doris Day's Let the Little Girl Limbo, written by Barry Mann and Cynthia Weil, was recorded in 1963 but didn't reach the public's ears till 1997; I first heard it on an album from the series of rescued pop music from the Columbia vaults, Where the Girls Are (Vol. 5). Ady Fidelin, Man Ray's lover at the time of the photograph taken by Roland

Penrose of Miller, Carrington, Eluard and her, was a dancer; she went on to become the first black model to feature not just in Harper's Bazaar (1937) but (according to a 2007 New York Times article) in any major fashion magazine. Nusch Eluard, an artist and performer in her own right, was the poet Paul Eluard's wife; she and her husband, members of the Resistance during the Second World War, were hounded by the Gestapo, and Nusch (whose fragility and malnutrition after the pressure of the war can clearly be seen in Lee Miller's late photos of her) died in 1946 at the age of forty. The famous Kafka quote comes from his letter to Oskar Pollak, January 27, 1904; Hitchcock talks about his plate-glass floor/ceiling and his thoughts on the whodunnit in a 1966 Granada tv program called Cinema, introduced by Mike Scott; the story of Dalí diving comes from Antony Penrose's 2001 book about his father, Roland Penrose: The Friendly Surrealist; the Hopkins lines come from the sonnet whose first line is 'No worst, there is none. Pitched past pitch of grief.' Edwin Morgan's Orphean poem is part iii of a poem called Rider, from his 1973 collection, From Glasgow to Saturn; Katherine Mansfield wrote about writing and acid in a letter to John Middleton Murry on May 19, 1913 and jotted down Robert Louis Stevenson's phrase 'literary vagrancy' in her notebooks; Stevenson suggested arriving was a lesser experience than traveling hopefully in 1881, in Virginibus Pueresque; and the Elizabeth Hardwick quote comes from her novel Sleepless Nights. The Greek myth about the musician in hopeless competition with Apollo is the story of Marsyas; the description of the Michelangelo drawing is of his Il Sogno (c. 1533); the Werner Herzog documentary about Chauvet is called Cave of Forgotten Dreams (2010). I owe a big thank-you to Artemis Loi, who kindly helped with all things Greek.

## On offer and on reflection

The Tove Jansson story is The Golden Calf, and is the first story in her 1968 short story collection, Bildhuggarens Dotter, translated into English in 1969 as Sculptor's Daughter. I hope Casanova *did* actually say this thing about women and pleasure; the only source I can find for it (apart from a 1984 book called Taking It Like a Woman by Ann Oakley, where it also appears to have been quoted) is the novel I first read it in, Elizabeth Hardwick's Sleepless Nights; because of this, I can't credit a translator, but I can send readers to this Hardwick novel and that's another pleasure in the handshake between sources. Jan Verwoert's comments on Giorgio Agamben, art, and profanity come from Frieze, Issue 129, March 2010. An aside: if I think of a contemporary inheritor of this fused literary force of coincidence/generosity found in the work of Dickens and Shakespeare, it's Kate Atkinson. The two song lines here about the cup o' tea for all are from Lionel Bart's Consider Yourself; the writer whose work first suggested to me this confluence of notions of kindness and family in the word kind is Sebastian Barry; the combination is one of the driving forces of his fiction, drama, and poetry. The Marlowe translation of the Ovid Elegy is from Elegy 8: He curses the bawd who has been instructing his mistress in the arts of a whore. The story goes that Marlowe's translation of Ovid's Elegies of Love, done in the early 1580s when he was still an undergraduate at Cambridge, was thought so 'unsemely' by the Archbishop of Canterbury when published that it was banned and burned. All my dictionary definitions throughout these talks come from The Chambers 20th and 21st Century Dictionaries; the Michael Ondaatje quote comes from The Cat's Table (2011); I found the Oscar Wilde story (which Wilde called The

Disciple) in Richard Ellmann's 1987 biography; the Atwood quote about Alice and the mirror is from Negotiating with the Dead; George Mackay Brown talked about the leafing of the imagination in an aside in an article about short story writing in the Orcadian, December 1983; David Constantine allowed me to quote from a piece he was writing, at the time of these lectures, about the crucial purpose and workings of the humanities (in an era where the fact that studying the humanities has to be rhetorically and economically justified tells us a great deal about contemporary state, mind-set, and philosophy); last of all, the piece about the thread of these adventures nearing its end is from a page or two before the close of Dickens's Oliver Twist.

# Permissions

**Picture Credits**

Jane Austen's Fiction Manuscripts: A Digital Edition www
.janeausten.ac.uk. Used by permission. With thanks to the
Bodleian Library Image Services Department.

'Studies for a Virgin and Child,' by Michelangelo © The
Trustees of the British Museum.

'Jupiter und Io,' by Antonio Allegri, called Correggio ©
Kunsthistorisches Museum, Vienna.

'Four Women Asleep,' Lee Miller, Leonora Carrington,
Ady Fidelin, Nusch Eluard, Lambe Creek, Cornwall,
England, 1937, by Roland Penrose © Roland Penrose Estate,
England 2012. The Roland Penrose Collection. All rights
reserved.

'Pastoral', by Leonora Carrington © ARS, NY and DACS, London 2012. With thanks to Susan Aberth for her help in sourcing the image.

Actress Aliki Vougiouklaki from the movie 'Punishment Came from Heaven' by Finos Film, 1959, Greece. With kind permission from Yiannis Papamichail, the son of Aliki Vougiouklaki.

Mercury, from Pompeii, c.50–79 AD (fresco), Roman, (1st century AD) / Museo Archeologico Nazionale, Naples, Italy / Giraudon / The Bridgeman Art Library.

'Autumn Tree,' 'Winter Tree,' 'Spring Tree,' and 'Summer Tree,' by Sarah Pickstone. With warm thanks to Sarah for her permission to use the paintings in this book.

**Text Permissions**

'Not Waving but Drowning,' by Stevie Smith, copyright (c) Estate of James MacGibbon, by permission.

'Not Marble: A Reconstruction,' by Edwin Morgan from *Collected Poems*. 1990. Used by permission of Carcanet Press Limited.